How Can I
Possibly
Forgive?

SARA HORN

HARVEST HOUSE PUBLISHERS
EUGENE, OREGON

Cover design by Dugan Design Group, Bloomington, Minnesota

Cover photo © BLOOM / Getty Images

Author photo © Michelle Bruton

The author is represented by the literary agency of Alive Communications, Inc., 7680 Goddard Street, Suite 200, Colorado Springs, CO 80920. www.alivecommunications.com.

HOW CAN I POSSIBLY FORGIVE?
Copyright © 2014 by Sara Horn
Published by Harvest House Publishers
Eugene, Oregon 97402
www.harvesthousepublishers.com

Library of Congress Cataloging-in-Publication Data
Horn, Sara, 1977-
How can I possibly forgive? / Sara Horn.
    pages cm
ISBN 978-0-7369-6099-1 (pbk.)
ISBN 978-0-7369-6100-4 (eBook)
1. Forgiveness—Religious aspects—Christianity. 2. Forgiveness of sin. I. Title.
BV4647.F55H67 2014
241'.4—dc23
                                                              2014010020

Printed in the United States of America

14 15 16 17 18 19 20 21 22 23 / VP-JH / 10 9 8 7 6 5 4 3 2 1

To those closest in my life,
who love me despite my flaws and
support me even when I make mistakes…
you have all played a part in helping me
learn about forgiveness.
This book is dedicated to you.

Acknowledgments

I am always grateful for the opportunities I'm given as a writer to share my words with others, but I certainly do not do it on my own.

Thank you to the Harvest House team for letting me be a part of your family. To Barb and LaRae, who knew a blog post could turn into 60,000 words? Thanks for encouraging me to pursue this topic. To Rod, my faithful friend and editor, thank you for your encouragement and expert editing.

Thank you to Andrea Heinecke, my agent, and the entire team at Alive Communications. I'm grateful for the many years (and books) we've now shared together.

To my amazing husband, Cliff—you have taught me so much about unconditional love. Thank you for loving me and for all the support you've given me. I love you, and I'm so happy you are home!

How Can I
Possibly
Forgive?

Contents

1

Listening Through the Noise

stood in my office staring at the phone in my hand. On the first ring I'd picked it up, but the name on the caller ID made me take a beat and pause. It was enough information to know my next few minutes were either going to be good—or not so good. OK, if they weren't good, they were probably about to be really, really unpleasant. Bad. Worse-than-going-to-your-dentist-for-multiple-root-canals uncomfortable.

Certain things run through your head when you're braced to have a difficult conversation with someone. I've found you can think about anything except what you really need to talk about, and there are a few popular choices we all tend to fall back on.

> Do I really even need to have this conversation?

The most obvious and the first one for many is *do I really even need to have this conversation?* After all, isn't there something more important I should do? Like clip my kid's fingernails (he's thirteen)? Or organize the dust bunnies under the bookshelves? Hang out with friends who *don't* require difficult conversations?

How to have a hard conversation or work through conflict with someone else isn't something they adequately prepare you for in school, except for maybe kindergarten, when you wanted the crayons to yourself and your teacher told you to share. I did go through an "intercommunications" class in college where the professor tried to teach us relational communication skills, but she seemed to spend the entire course with a rather large chip on her shoulder from somewhere that spilled over into her teaching and how she interacted with her students. I think I spent more time during that class thinking about the irony of that than how to successfully have a difficult conversation.

In high school I took a voluntary "peer mediation" course, which was the school's way of using good kids to help talk some sense into bad kids by "mediating" their problems so they could avoid yet another detention or suspension. We'd sit in small rooms in the school library with the door closed, one tough-looking kid on one side of a table, another equally tough kid on the other side, and us "good kids" in the middle. Our job was to instruct them to use magic phrases like "When you do this, I feel like this" and ask questions like "How did that make you feel?" and secretly hope neither kid decided to just join forces and take out their feelings on *us*.

But there is no set of guidelines or peer mediation manual to follow when you're dealing with conflict as an adult. There's no one sitting on a chair next to you, asking provoking questions to get you to open up (well, unless you pay for it), and there is no law that forces someone to talk something out with you.

There's another thought you think about when you're going head-to-head with someone: *How do I win this discussion? How do I get my way on this issue?* You think through all the tactics you learned when you were on the debate team—or at least that time your teacher made you take part in a mock debate and asked you to defend why "homework is good for you," which is a very mean thing to do to a fourth grader, if you think about it. (Your street cred will never be the same.) You think about the arguments that will support why you're right—and why the other person's wrong. You come up with statements that acknowledge something about where the other person is coming from, but twist it so it's impossible for them to do anything but agree you were right. When you're ready to talk to someone to resolve a disagreement, or hard feelings, or any issue life is known to bring up—it's tempting to just want to win more than you want to shake hands and play nice (though maybe not as helpful longterm).

But there's also another thought you might have.

Will she say she's sorry? Will he admit he was wrong?

Will she say she's sorry? Will he admit he was wrong?

Pain is involved here. True, genuine hurt. Words said or actions taken that wounded you deeply, and all you want—all you're looking for—is a little relief from the pain and an apology as a good start. You might also debate the merits of apologizing yourself, since chances are good if they did something to you, you did something to them. What would be the harm in just moving forward together, with a fresh start?

The Phone Call to Nowhere

The phone rang again. I took a deep breath. My mind ran through all the issues with this person over the last several months. We'd never sat down and talked anything out, although I'd tried a couple of times, but plenty was said to other people, some of it getting back to me. I only knew from the complaints and accusations I'd heard through secondhand sources that she was frustrated with me, and from my perspective, didn't like me very much. I also had my own frustrations to sort out—things that were done that, to me, felt like slights and inconsiderate choices and, in some cases, just wrong. Hard feelings had built to distracting crescendos in my brain.

I knew I couldn't just write her out of my life, though the idea was tempting.

Though I don't like dealing with conflict any more than others, I knew I couldn't just write her out of my life, though the idea was tempting some days. I sincerely wanted things to get better between us. I knew that's what God wanted. But knowing and doing can sometimes feel like trying to jump over the Grand Canyon.

The phone rang again. I hit "Talk."

"Hey, Sara, I heard you wanted to talk about something? What's going on?"

Her question stumped me a bit. I knew exactly what was going on. We weren't getting along. We weren't even really talking. There was a whole lot of complaining and fussing happening under the surface, and I was tired of the tension and the drama.

I took another breath. "Well, I just thought we needed to talk some things out. You seem to be upset about some things, I'm upset about some things, we've just kind of let things build up, and I wanted to get it all out in the open so we can resolve what's been bugging us and so we can have a good relationship moving forward."

> Putting yourself out there never feels good. When you make yourself vulnerable, it's scary.

Now I was holding my breath. Putting yourself out there never feels good. When you make yourself vulnerable, it's scary, even when trying to offer a peace offering. But I took the chance. I'd swatted that ball over the net. Now I waited for the return.

All I heard was silence. My heart beat faster, the way it does when something I don't want to happen is about to. Fight or flight was in full force, and it took everything for me not to just end the conversation right then. I knew she was about to say some things I probably would disagree with—things from her perspective I didn't see at all—but I was ready to listen. I was ready to do my best to smooth things over so we could move on and have a good friendship.

"There's nothing wrong," she said. "I don't have a problem with you."

Well, everything I've heard says you do, I thought. *Your actions say you do too.* Another breath. *Let's try this again.*

"What about…" I brought up some of the specific things I knew she'd complained about to others, things I'd done or said that bothered her. I brought up things she'd done that hurt my feelings. There were misunderstandings. We'd both been oversensitive. I felt like I'd tried to offer olive branches at different times, and got no response in return. But the more I tried to explain why we needed to talk, the more defensive she became. My own voice was getting louder.

We just have to talk this out, I thought. *No pain, no gain. Keep talking. Just keep talking. At least we're talking. That's a start.*

She made another attempt to get out of the conversation. "Look, I'm fine, there's nothing wrong. You may have a problem, but I don't."

Have you ever used that approach in a difficult conversation? That's a brilliant tactic, by the way. It puts all the issues, all the hard feelings, on the other person. It gets you out of the conversation because it implies you shouldn't even be *part of* the conversation (remember my first thought about even having the conversation?).

I could feel my frustration bubbling into anger, my face getting hot. "Really? There's nothing wrong? That's not what I'm hearing, and that's not what I'm getting from you when we're around each other. And if everything really is OK, than please stop telling other people you're upset with me or what you don't like about—hello? Hello?"

She'd hung up. For two minutes, we'd talked. I called back and got her voicemail and left her a message, asking her to return my call. A little while later, I got a voicemail

> Relationships are messy. People are messy.

from her, though my phone never rang. She said she'd dropped her phone. Asked me to call her back. I called back. Left another voicemail. Told her I still wanted to talk. Even though we've seen each other countless times since then in different group settings, I'm still waiting for that conversation. For some people, staying at the surface of a relationship is as far as they're comfortable going.

I know I'm not the only one who has ever gone through a struggle with a friend or a family member. Relationships are messy. People are messy. Finding a way to navigate through all the feelings, intentions, relating and nonrelating, agendas and nonagendas can be exhausting. We don't always learn how to cope as well as we might.

When I was growing up, I had two distinctly different examples to go by when it came to conflict in relationships. My father's side of the family and my mother's.

My dad's family all lived in the West, mainly in California, and because our family lived mostly in the South and Northeast, I didn't see them much. My father's mother passed away before my dad ever met my mom, so I never knew my paternal grandmother, and I can count on one hand the number of times I saw my grandfather. For a brief time, my family lived in Washington state when I was in first and second grade, and I remember us taking a visit to see my grandfather in his ranch-style home somewhere in the Napa Valley and playing with his big German shepherd who loved stretching out underneath a long wooden table in the dining room.

I remember my grandfather's kind eyes that twinkled a little when he smiled, and though he was quiet, he seemed like a nice man, someone I wish I could have known better. One year he visited us in our home in Louisiana and brought Care Bears to my brother and sister and me. He'd remarried sometime before I was born, to a woman named Francois, with a thick Swiss accent and even thicker hair she wore up on her head. I still have a little plastic Swiss doll my grandfather gave me, as well as an old crèche that makes me think of him every year when I pull it out for Christmas.

But growing up and living away, the communication was minimal with my grandfather and my dad's siblings (my aunt and uncles), and my mom was the one who usually called and kept in touch. She'd catch up on jobs and life and what my grandfather and his wife and everyone else were doing. But I never felt that connection. When he passed away two years after Cliff and I got married, a wedding he hadn't attended, I cried hard in my husband's arms, not as much for my grandfather's passing but for the man I never really got to know.

My mother's family was the opposite of my dad's. Mom was from North Carolina, and since we lived a lot closer, we had more opportunity to travel and see her family for visits. What I remember most about those visits was the food. Southerners talk with their skillets. My mom's grandmother would make platter after platter of scrambled eggs and fried sausage and fluffy biscuits with white gravy and golden-brown hash browns, and I remember hearing my mom's laugh carry across the small house as she visited with her favorite granny in the kitchen she remembered visiting often as a child.

But visits with other family members weren't always so fun or enjoyable. Mom's family didn't have a problem talking, and while she had cousins who were sweet and kind, conversations among other family members could turn into full-scale arguments before lunch ever got put on the table. Someone always seemed to be angry or upset or down with a case of the hurt feelings. Though I was too young to understand it all then, I suspected there were scars that ran deep and hurts that never quite found healing.

I hated how a visit upset and stressed my mother and made my dad quieter than he already was—if he actually came, which wasn't often. He usually stayed home and worked. As a result of those memories, when I got older, I too avoided those visits if I could help it.

> You can't be bothered with the messiness of relationships and hard feelings if you never really have time for them.

Avoiding negative stuff or negative people was something I learned to do early on. Since

I didn't like dealing with the negative, I poured myself into activity, usually of the positive variety. You can't be bothered with the messiness of relationships and hard feelings if you never really have time for them.

As a high school student, I started clubs and organizations and causes and participated in so many things, the yearbook editors had to ask me to shorten my senior profile because they ran out of room. But friendships with the other students who helped in those groups were a second thought. I seemed to care more about the project than the person, maybe because it felt safer.

In college, my busy-bee ways slowed down just enough so I could discover and fall in love with my husband. But after we married, I got back into my old habits, consuming myself with work and goals and accomplishment. Dealing with work or the day-to-day came easy. Checking off a project was something I could control. Handling and managing the rolling, changing-by-the-day emotions of other people was much harder—and hardly controllable.

> Deciding to no longer hold a grudge toward someone is just the beginning of what has to happen when we're talking about forgiveness.

So for me, at least for a long time, accomplishment replaced relationship because—as we've established—relationships were messy. They never ended like an episode of your favorite nineties' sitcom, where a conflict resolved itself in forty-five minutes or less, and you always knew everything was going to be OK when the music swelled and people hugged.

I wish relationships could be as easy as that. I wish forgiveness could happen that easily all the time. But for a lot of us, saying "I'm sorry" or deciding to no longer hold a grudge toward someone or something is just the beginning of what has to happen when we're talking about forgiveness.

It's Complicated

So, yes, relationships are messy. People are complicated. As women, we are definitely complicated.

In my early twenties, when I worked in the corporate world, it was easier working with the men than the women, at least that's how I felt at the time. Men were straightforward; women, with the rare exception, not so much. Men cared about *what* you did on the job; women cared *how* you did your job along with everything else (and weren't afraid to tell you). Even after God called me into women's ministry and led me to start a ministry for military wives, I was reluctant because when I thought about working with women, I thought of the complicated drama that might unfold. Hard feelings forming quicker than a look someone didn't like. Women who might bring ongoing issues with them that never seemed to—well—*go* anywhere. (Do you know women in your life like this? You want to love them like Jesus, but sometimes you just want to send them to Jesus!)

In some much-needed quiet time with the Lord shortly after my phone call that went nowhere with my friend, I read Proverbs 10:12. "Hatred stirs up conflicts, but love covers all offenses." The verse hit me deeply, because I knew I was getting more and more bitter toward the situation. The commentary in my study Bible brought the point home. "Loving people, unlike hateful ones, are willing to put up with insults or slander and to forgive those who wrong them."

> Go ahead, put up with insults. Forgive those who wrong you. These aren't statements we find in our Facebook news feeds.

Go ahead, put up with insults. Forgive those who wrong you. These aren't statements we find on the back of our boxes of cereal or in our Facebook news feeds. We're much more likely to hear that we need to take a stand, shake the dust off, and worry about ourselves before we worry about anyone else. We're better than they are. We don't need them.

But is that an attitude of love? Is this what people who love do? Is this what followers of Christ, who should fit in the category of people who love, do?

Forgiveness isn't just ignoring bad behavior (though I think we're tempted to see it that way sometimes). Making the choice to act like we don't see or care when we really do isn't the answer either. A friend shared this quote with me the other day from Tony Evans, a pastor and author, who said that forgiveness isn't "pretending like it didn't happen or like it didn't hurt. That's called lying. Forgiveness is a decision to release a debt regardless of how you feel."

It also isn't about putting up with wrongs and acting like it's no big deal, while in the back of your mind you secretly keep a list of what's been done. That's like keeping some weird version of a voodoo doll with you and sticking a mental pin in every time that memory comes back to hurt you. The problem is, the only person really feeling any pain is you.

No, forgiveness is an act of letting something go. Letting that wrong, letting that unresolved issue, letting that person who always seems to know the exact thing to say to hurt you or frustrate you—letting all of it fade away.

Jesus makes it pretty clear that forgiveness isn't just about us. He has a lot of interest in whether we pass on the gift of grace to someone else. In Matthew 6:14-15, he tells his disciples, "if you forgive people their wrongdoing, your heavenly Father will forgive you as well. But if you don't forgive people, your Father will not forgive your wrongdoing."

> We have to release the debt.

He makes this statement immediately after sharing his guide for praying. There's that little sentence in what we know as the Lord's Prayer so many of us grew up reciting that says, "Forgive us our debts, as we also have forgiven our debtors."

Forgive us for what we owe. Forgive us where we come up short. Forgive us where we lack. Jesus makes the point that if we are so eager and OK in coming to him for our forgiveness, we have to willingly offer the same to others. We have to release the debt.

That Jesus talks about forgiveness when he talks about prayer is also a reminder we don't just need to forgive, but to also pray for those who hurt us. In Matthew 5:44-45, Jesus tells us to love our enemies and pray for those who persecute us, "so that you may be sons of your Father in heaven." That's an important connection Jesus shows us—the unconditional love he gives us is what he asks us to give others.

To really appreciate that unconditional love—God's grace I am so grateful for every day that he gives us when we don't deserve it—we need a better understanding of forgiveness. We don't always notice it right away or see it easily. I can't take out a special tool that allows me to look into the hearts of others. I can't analyze where that person is on the spectrum of being humble and sorry or just being defiant and a jerk. But I do think we can hear when forgiveness is present and when it's not. I think we begin understanding this whole idea of forgiveness when we start listening—to ourselves, to others, and to God (and not necessarily in that order).

Women often write me about the struggles they go through with others, the mess that is life sometimes. Some have hearts that have hardened, women who aren't letting go of their hurt and pain and just want to give up altogether. I get it. I've been there.

Identifying the White Noise in Your Life

There have been seasons in my life when I've let the white noise of bitterness and frustration and self-doubt drown out any other sound the Lord wanted me to hear. Do you know what I mean? That static sound that always runs in the background? We listen to

> What distracts our hearts distracts our souls.

this white noise as it settles in our hearts, reminding, condemning, and distracting us by repeating over and over in our minds the hurts, the pain, the offenses, the slights that have been done to you and me. It isn't always loudly noticeable—sometimes it's quite subtle—but it's there, and this is what I've learned from that noise: *what distracts our hearts distracts our souls.* What keeps us tied to that mocking sound, whispering who or what has done us wrong, keeps us from hearing God's soothing voice telling us what we must do. How we should handle the hurt. What we can say. What we need to do with our next step. Sometimes, what we need to say in our next sentence.

Can you identify any of these white N-O-I-S-Es in your life?

Negative Self-Talk

"You'll never fix this." "You'll always be this way." "You are such a failure." I think this is one of the most common noises we hear when we're struggling to forgive ourselves after making wrong choices or bad judgments. But these aren't just negative statements we let penetrate our hearts. These are lies. Isaiah 43:19 says,

> "Look, I am about to do something new;
>   even now it is coming. Do you not see it?
> Indeed, I will make a way in the wilderness,
>   rivers in the desert."

When you believe that nothing can ever change in yourself or in others, you will never see the importance of forgiving yourself or someone else. Forgiveness offers second chances and a hope for change. I know in my own life, Jesus constantly takes my doubts, my mistakes, my trip ups, and my screwups and allows me to try again. He makes a way. There is always an opportunity to make something better. We learn from our mistakes and failures, and whatever today has brought, we know tomorrow can be brand-new. So stop telling yourself, "I can't" or "I'll never be" or "I never will." Instead, replace those words with these: Jesus can…Jesus always is…Jesus will…

Other People's Opinions

As women, we have a lot of opinions, don't we? And we especially value our own! But we also want to know what others think. The problem comes when we don't like those opinions—or we don't know what to do with them when they don't exactly mesh with ours.

> She'd let that woman's words penetrate her heart and dissolve into noise that wouldn't leave.

I have a sweet friend who once helped me start a local group for military wives. None of the ladies who came to our first meeting really knew each other, and so we took turns introducing ourselves. My friend shared a story of the day she felt God called her to go into nursing school. One of the other women, an older, much more outspoken lady, was quick to offer her opinion, and it wasn't a very encouraging one (although it wasn't intended to be discouraging either, I don't think). Though I didn't pay much attention to it at the time, my friend later posted a very self-defeating message on her Facebook page, and I knew that woman's words had stung her. She was hurt, she felt deflated, and as far as I know, she never applied for nursing school. She also wasn't part of the group for much longer. She'd let that woman's words penetrate her heart and dissolve into noise that wouldn't leave.

When we allow other people's opinions into our hearts as truth instead of as thoughts that we have a choice to accept or dismiss, we establish the foundation of walls God doesn't want in our lives. We hold on to things we don't need to hold on to. Other people's opinions fit into that category.

Inconsiderate Friends and Family

This is a tough one, right? My husband and I sometimes share a familiar saying when we're finding ourselves a little frustrated on the family front: "Fish and family are a lot alike; it takes about three days before they both start going bad." When I think about family, I think about a safe place where you can be yourself. But sometimes that backfires on you. Family members may say things to you they might never say to a friend or to someone at church or to a stranger. I've found myself on the receiving end of those statements, and it's hard not to allow hard feelings to build up, one small hurt at a time.

> Family members may say things to you they might never say to a friend or to someone at church or to a stranger.

One of my best friends has also been hurt in similar situations, and we use each other as a sounding board, offering reminders to the other that what's been said isn't necessarily truth. If you're not careful, those slights and undeserved remarks can take up a low hum, staying with you, always in the background, in a never-ending loop.

Stingers

These are the harshest of white noise and they can go back a long way. They're the words said when you were a kid that you've never forgotten. Sometimes it's the way they were said and how they made you feel in the moment. They hurt. They crush. They make you shrink back in defeat. They can start the beginning of resentment that takes such deep root, you aren't even aware of it sometimes because you've lived with this noise in your head for so long.

I still remember the words of my sophomore science teacher in high school, Mr. Walters. Mr. Walters was a short, stout little man with a fuzzy moustache and a big gruff voice. His nickname for me was "Bowlbs," a shortened version of my maiden name. Since I sat in one of the front desks, he always seemed to be in front of me, barking out his lesson for the day. Every once in a while, just for amusement, he'd bark, "Ain't that right, Bowlbs?" I didn't really know what to make of him, whether he liked me or not. The chemistry class was hard for me, and before the first nine weeks were over, I was called down to the guidance office. Sitting at her desk, my counselor barely looked up from the papers in front of me as she dropped the news.

"Sara, I noticed you have a *C* in your chemistry class," she said. "This early in the school year, that's a concern, and so I talked with your teacher and asked him what he thought. He said he has no hope for you and you should think about a remedial class, one that isn't as advanced."

> As I sat there, taking in what she was telling me, I refused to let my teacher's words define me.

He has no hope for you.

Just thinking about those words today still stings. My stomach hurt, and I felt angry that someone was so quick to give up on me. As I sat there, taking in what she was telling me, I refused to let my teacher's words define me. Instead, I let them challenge me, and I told my counselor in the politest terms possible that Mr. Walters didn't know what he was talking about, and I would stay in his class and I would pass it. And that's what I did. The year was hard, and there were struggles and tears, but acing the final exam in that class made up for all of it.

Still, that stinger has stayed with me into adulthood and has probably contributed in some small part to the feeling that I always need to prove myself. You may have words that have stayed with you too.

Elevated Problem

This type of noise is a combination of some of the other noises in your head, where hurtful comments or ongoing conflict grow in your mind and heart bigger and faster than Alice did when she ate the cake that said "Eat Me." It feels impossible to let go, because the pressure of this noise feels enormous and constant. You constantly think about it. You now avoid a friend who hurt your feelings to the point you'll leave an event or a gathering early, or not go at all if you know she's going to be there. A relative's phone calls get ignored thanks to caller ID. (Be honest—how many phone numbers are in your cell phone specifically so if they ever call, you know not to answer?)

Sometimes this noise extends beyond just individuals. Something someone said or didn't say to you at church morphs into discouragement or anger about the *whole church*, and you change churches or quit going altogether. A work issue that unfairly put you in a bad light keeps you from looking at your coworkers who didn't back you up without thinking about that situation and the hard feelings it caused. Every...single...time.

> When I gave my life to Christ, it was a commitment to completely surrender my will for his.

If there's a lesson I've learned through the experiences and journeys God has taken me on over the last few years, it's that my life is not my own. That lesson certainly applies when we're talking about forgiveness. When I gave my life to Christ, it wasn't a deal where I said OK and God would step in and make my wildest dreams come true—not at all. When I gave my life to Christ, it was a commitment to completely surrender my will for his. That includes overlooking hurts and the grievances that happen from other people.

I don't think God expects us to just roll over like a lamb, though. Talking things out is healthy and important and helps relationships and friendships grow. But if someone isn't willing to do that, then you're not left with a whole lot of other options.

Except to forgive that person anyway.

A New Sound

I'm tired of letting this white noise—these negative thoughts and feelings—capture and distract my attention from the better things God is calling me to. Aren't you? If you've picked up this book, chances are you're ready to start tuning out some of this noise you've allowed to keep you from a more peaceful life, a more joyful living. But let's be real here. Some things in your life you've tried to let go—you've tried to forgive and move on—and so far it hasn't happened. We're talking painful stuff, not just the petty. Deep, lingering wounds and scars you've prayed for years that God would close up and heal so you can move on with your life. But God may already be working on those scars, on that healing. He's just waiting for you to meet him halfway.

In many of the miracles we read about in the Bible, Jesus uses people in the process. When Mary, his mother, asked him to fix the wine shortage at the wedding, Jesus asked the servants to bring him six sizable stone water jars before he changed the water into something more suitable for a celebration. When the disciples were in the boat and no fish could be found, Jesus asked them to hurl out their nets on the other side before they found the fish. Before Jesus brought Lazarus out of the tomb, he asked for men, presumably the friends and family of Lazarus, to move back the stone covering.

Jesus may be asking something of you today as he prepares to heal your heart, as he helps you let go and get ready to move on from the things keeping you from living the fuller life he desires for you.

> Experiencing the ability to truly forgive and let go can come only when we're intentional.

Who is it he wants you to forgive?

What is he asking you to let go of?

What have you tied yourself down with, and insisted on carrying, that he wants you to leave behind?

I wish I could say everything we discuss in this book will give you the answers you need to finally do just that. Sometimes, though, the scars, the hurts, can't be healed with just a few thoughts, a few chapters you read with coffee in hand. Experiencing the ability to truly forgive and let go can come only when we're intentional, when we bring our pain and our struggle to forgive, our difficulty to move beyond what's keeping us stuck—when we bring it all to

God in prayer and ask him to work through our efforts to change, our attempts to let go.

Even after doing that, you may still need to sit down and talk more with someone: a close friend who's also a good listener, a pastor, or a Christian counselor. Don't wait. Don't try to justify or make excuses for why you don't need to or why you can't. The sooner you face what you've tried to avoid, the sooner you can hear what forgiveness really sounds like.

My prayer is that something you read as we spend some time together will help further you toward finally finding peace and the ability to forgive whoever or whatever has hurt you. I'm praying as I write this that the sound you hear is the sound of relief as you experience, maybe for the first time, what it feels like to truly forgive and let go.

So let's stop listening to the noise and start listening for God's voice. Let's let go of the junk and grab on to his truth. Let's move on to the plans God has for you and refuse to let bitterness or undercurrents of hard feelings get in the way.

Are you ready?

Five Ways to Start Forgiving Right Now

1. **Pray for the person who wounded you.** Ask God for insight and understanding into this person's life and for the situation you're challenged with.

2. **Look the offending person in the eye, say hello, and offer a compliment.** It's easier to hold on to grudges and hard feelings when you pretend the other person doesn't exist. It's not as easy when you have to be reminded they're human just like you. Whether they respond in kind doesn't matter. What matters is what you do.

3. **Do the right thing.** Whether someone is willing to meet you halfway or not, do what is right and don't worry about what the other person is doing or not doing.

4. **Be OK with what you've got.** Sometimes problems develop because our expectations are higher than what someone else is willing to give or be. When you've done what you can to bring a relationship closer, but there's no movement from the other side, there's not a lot more you can do. Accept what you have and look at the close relationships you do have and be grateful for them.

5. **Pick your battles.** Choose peace over winning. This is hard. Especially if the person you're struggling with makes no effort to change whatever behavior hurt you in the first place. But respond to insults with kindness. Show smiles to slights and huffs. Remind yourself you've already been bought with a price, and your peace doesn't come from someone who doesn't see the value in you anyway. It comes from Christ. So focus on him.

2

Letting Go of the Hurt

This past year my family got a new addition to the household. Lucy, a one-year-old, white, floppy-eared miniature schnauzer joined us. Sammy, our eight-year-old, salt-and-pepper schnauzer, has been with us since he was six months old, and we thought he could use the company of a second dog. They could play together, be a companion for each other—we just knew it would be a great relationship.

I wish I could say it has gone that way.

People say no two kids are the same, and no two dogs are the same, either. Where Sammy's demeanor has always been that of a laid-back, friendly, and all-around good dog, Lucy is not turning out that way. She's super hyper. She hasn't responded to our training as quickly as Sammy did. Her shrill, high-pitched bark announces when anyone comes near the house or to the door. She's a pack rat. She steals things from low-level tables or from under beds and hides them behind one specific couch. She chews up paper, gnaws caps off water bottles, and eats Caleb's homework. (Yes, that is a legitimate excuse in our house since Lucy came.) She's also destroyed our son's glasses—twice.

As I wrote this section today, I had a minor crisis with my laptop. The cord failed and stopped charging my battery, and with only about 8 percent power left, I ran out for ten minutes to buy a replacement. In my hurry, I failed to "Lucy-proof" the house, and in the short time I was gone, she managed to destroy a speaking agreement I didn't pick up before I left. I think she was misnamed. Shredder might have been more appropriate.

Lucy has only two modes of operation—high speed and asleep. When she's awake, she flies around the house like a launched missile, and if you don't pay attention to her, she whines the most awful dying-cow moan you've ever heard. I'm serious. Imagine a cow mooing its final moo on this earth, and that's what Lucy sounds like.

> Lucy has only two modes of opera-tion—high speed and asleep.

None of those issues come close to her biggest problem, though. Lucy is one jealous female dog. If someone pets Sammy, Lucy pushes him out of the way so she can be the one to get the scratch behind the ears. If we give them both treats, Lucy almost swallows hers whole so she can grab at least part of Sammy's before he's finished.

Because Lucy still hasn't completely warmed up to the idea of house training (we find a gift about every two or three weeks where it shouldn't be), we keep her in her crate at night. She's not a fan. Usually we have to bribe her with an ice cube (she loves ice) or with a little piece of a dog biscuit to get her to come. When we do this, all we have to say is "crate," and she torpedoes her way there in a flat two seconds, waiting for her reward.

I'd prefer her to just come when we call her, though, and so one night, I stood near her crate and attempted to get her to come of her own free will. She sat in the doorway of the kitchen and looked at me from across the living room, paws firmly planted on the floor. So I did the first thing that came to my mind.

"Sammy! Come here, Sammy!"

Not exactly a young pup anymore, Sammy's head was just lifting from his resting place on the couch when a white blur of fur hurled across the fifteen feet of flooring, skidded into the crate, and looked up at me expectantly as I shook my head and shut the crate door in her face.

I admit it. I couldn't help but feel a strong sense of satisfaction as I thought, *Sucker*. OK, I might have said that out loud too. I mentioned she's chewed up Caleb's glasses twice, right? She and I have a love-hate relationship, and the jury is still out on which one it is.

Since that night, I've thought a lot about how that little dog responded to my calling Sammy instead of her. She was so concerned about someone else getting something she wasn't, in her eagerness to ensure that didn't happen, she put herself in the very box she hated. She shut herself in. She put herself in a corner of her own making.

> She was so concerned about someone else getting something she wasn't, she put herself in the very box she hated.

Don't we do that to ourselves when we resent other people? We get so worried with our own insecurities, so caught up and concerned about our personal inadequacies—of coming up short or someone else getting something we don't have—that a person can just look at us wrong and we hold a grudge. Women are really good at this. We clutch hard feelings tighter than a Coach purse on a sales rack. And those feelings can start early.

I remember the frustrations and sourness I had toward a friend in high school. Even as a freshman, Jenni got a leading role *every single time* in our school's fall play or spring musical. By our junior year, after I was relegated to the orchestra pit as a backup singer and watched her cast yet again as the lead, this time as Dorothy in our version of *The Wiz*, I became convinced our choir director was handpicking shows specifically for her. It was hard not to see her in the hall without a big ol' bucket of strong dislike forming in the pit of my stomach. The worst part was that she wasn't even mean. She didn't lord her "don't hate me because I'm talented and I get picked for everything" persona over anyone. She was sweet and caring and kind.

I remember the enormous wave of guilt that washed over me the day we found out who was going to be the female lead for the spring musical our senior year. I'd spent the entire summer preparing for the audition. I'd practiced the part, over and over, and finally the day came when I stood in front of that cast list and stared at my name, which was right next to the lead female character's name. I couldn't believe the feeling of simultaneous excitement and disbelief. *I got it. I finally got a leading role.*

> I had missed out on what might have been a great friendship because I let my jealousy trap me and keep me in a vise of resentment.

Jenni walked up, looked for herself, and with a sweet sincere smile said, "Congratulations, Sara!" and gave me a hug. No dislike. No sarcasm. No visible anger. I realized I had missed out on what might have been a great friendship because I let my jealousy (and one big whopper of a grudge that she didn't deserve) trap me and keep me in a vise of resentment.

Someone once said that resentment is like drinking poison and waiting for the other person to die. When we care more about our hard feelings than what God might want for us in a specific relationship, we do poison ourselves. We contaminate hearts that are supposed to be set apart for God, because how can they be set apart if they're focused on things that aren't for him or of him? We know 1 Corinthians 13 as the Love chapter, and we know we need to be patient and kind (v. 4). But I think sometimes we miss the part that says love "is not irritable or resentful; it does not rejoice at wrongdoing, but rejoices with the truth" (1 Corinthians 13:5-6 ESV).

So what does it look like when you're caught up in resentment and you may not even know it? How do you eradicate it from your life? What can you replace it with?

Let's look at Seven Habits of Highly Resentful People—and compare those with the Seven Habits of Highly Forgiving People.

As you read through these, ask which habits you need to let go and which ones you need to practice.

Seven Habits of Highly Resentful People

1. A highly resentful person never stops grumbling.

Do you remember the story of the Israelites starting in the book of Exodus? God's people were slaves to Pharaoh until he used Moses to lead them out. But even after being rescued, they found reason to complain. They grumbled about the living conditions in the wilderness, they fussed about food and water, and when a group came back with an intimidating report on Canaan, the land God had promised to his people, they moaned and resented God himself. "If only we had died in the land of Egypt, or if only we had died in this wilderness! Why is the LORD bringing us into this land to die by the sword?...Let's appoint a leader and go back to Egypt" (Numbers 14:2-4).

> When you practice grumbling, more grumbling is sure to follow.

We're not talking about whether someone sees the proverbial glass half full or empty. When you practice grumbling, more grumbling is sure to follow. When we stop looking for the good, all we see is the bad. If you find yourself in an ongoing pattern of grumbling, remember Paul's words in Philippians: "Do everything without grumbling and arguing, so that you may be blameless and pure" (2:14-15a).

2. A highly resentful person always seems to be offended by something.

There's a lot of self-righteous thinking that happens when someone is habitually offended. So self-confident in her own abilities or her personal decisions or choices, if she's not careful, her confidence changes into feelings of superiority, where nothing is ever quite right because it's never quite good enough for her. A worship service is offensive because she didn't like a song the music minister chose. Someone doesn't speak to her and she feels slighted. She isn't asked to serve on a particular PTO committee at school. Snap judgments and negative first impressions also are part of the I'm Offended package.

The Pharisees were notorious for getting offended by Jesus, and the resentment they felt toward him only grew until they had him crucified. But Jesus didn't hold anything back when he told them what their problem was: "you have neglected the more important matters of the law—justice, mercy, and faith" (Matthew 23:23). We're more likely to be offended when we fall into the comfortable lie that we're sinless and deserving, and we forget we're unable to save ourselves. Only Jesus can.

3. A highly resentful person is constantly disappointed by others and by life in general.

Job speaks for a lot of us who have been disappointed by people and by life's circumstances, and sometimes even by God.

> But when I hoped for good, evil came;
> when I looked for light, darkness came.
> I am churning within and cannot rest;
> days of suffering confront me.
> (Job 30:26-27)

Disappointments are part of life. There are many legitimate, hurtful disappointments we face. There are also disappointments that come when we've placed higher expectations on someone or something than warranted. When we hold on to those disappointments, resentment can take hold of us. We stop being positive like Pooh and become much more cloudy in our attitude like Eeyore.

4. A highly resentful person is dissatisfied with some area of her life, if not several.

Have you ever met someone like this? They aren't much fun to be around. They're usually complaining about what's not right in their life or what they wish could change, but they're unwilling to do anything to make those changes. They're good at playing the blame game. They can feel rudderless, unable to control anything, and it's always someone else's fault, never theirs.

The sense of emptiness we often feel when we're dissatisfied with something should be a cue that our wholeness cannot come from ourselves. Only when we commit our lives to Christ can we experience full satisfaction because we know our joy and our gain don't come from anything the world can offer. Our satisfaction can come only from Christ.

> Only when we commit our lives to Christ can we experience full satisfaction.

The Samaritan woman Jesus met with at the well may have felt quite dissatisfied with her life. Nothing had happened the way she'd envisioned. But Jesus told her, "whoever drinks from the water that I will give him will never get thirsty again—ever! In fact, the water I will give him will become a well of water springing up within him for eternal life" (John 4:14).

5. A highly resentful person avoids spending time with God.

A resentful spirit cannot reside in your heart when God is active and working in your midst. When I am edgy and spiteful and just generally unpleasant to be around, it's usually because I haven't spent time reading God's Word or talking with him. Resentment births questions like, "What's in this for me?" instead of asking how God can be blessed or honored through us. Are we thinking horizontally or vertically? Are we thinking of ourselves, like the Israelites who "grumbled in their tents and did not listen to the Lord's voice" (Psalm 106:25), or are we thinking like Jesus? When we do the latter, resentment has no place to stay.

> A resentful spirit cannot reside in your heart when God is active and working in your midst.

6. *A highly resentful person is quick to get angry.*

Resentment is a breeding ground for bad tempers. One of the first cases we have of anger in the Bible is between Cain and Abel. Both brothers brought offerings to the Lord from their field and flock respectively, but God "had regard" only for Abel's offering (Genesis 4:4). The word *regard* means God accepted or paid attention only to Abel's, and Cain was furious. He had two things working against him—he was resentful of God's decision not to accept his gift, and he was jealous of his brother. Though God warned him about his dangerous attitude, Cain refused to listen (another habit of resentment), and he met his brother out in a field and killed him.

I doubt you've ever done anything as extreme as Cain, but you may have allowed your anger to kill a relationship or write off a friendship. Psalm 37:8 tells us to "refrain from anger and give up your rage; do not be agitated—it can only bring harm." If you know you have a short fuse, don't buy into the lie that this is just the way you are and the way you'll always be. Ecclesiastes 7:9 implores us not to let our spirits "rush to be angry, for anger abides in the heart of fools." There are so many better things to apply our strength and energy toward.

7. *A highly resentful person hangs on to pride.*

She will lie, gossip, and put others down before the reputation she's worked so hard to build is marred or damaged. For a long time this was me. Not necessarily the lying or the gossiping, but at least in my mind I put others down in order to feel better about myself. My value, my self-worth was caught up in what I did, so if someone else did something better, in my eyes my value was diminished. Resentment could pop up in my heart before I saw it coming. Only because of God's grace and his Word taking root in my life have I been able to put the pride down and recognize God's wise words spoken through Paul, to "do nothing out of rivalry or conceit, but in

Pride starts when insecurity peaks.

humility consider others as more important than yourselves" (Philippians 2:3).

If you struggle in this area, let me encourage you. Pride starts when insecurity peaks. Be secure in Christ. He loves you more than anyone or anything could possibly make you feel loved.

Seven Habits of Highly Forgiving People

1. A highly forgiving person is intentional about living in peace.

People with forgiving hearts don't usually live in a soap opera. Drama doesn't follow them around, and they don't chase it. Jesus gives us some clear instructions when it comes to forgiveness (Luke 6:27-28), though I'll be the first to admit, none of it is easy. Most of it requires stepping out of your comfort zone and letting go of your wants and your expectations. Love your enemies. Bless those who curse you. Pray for those who mistreat you. These are powerful actions that can produce peaceful results.

2. A highly forgiving person is kind. She cares more about doing the right thing in a given situation than what is in it for her.

This can be hard, but I think it's possible to practice kindness and get in a habit of it when you do it often enough. When we can see every person we come into contact with as someone Jesus loves, I think it's a little easier for us to show love as well. I've written about this before, but one of the first places we can learn to practice more kindness is in our marriages. So often we will be kind to a stranger before we're willing to show kindness to our spouses.

> When we make it a habit to give in other ways, it's not so hard to give grace and second chances as well.

Showing kindness means speaking gently toward others, offering help with the expectation of nothing in return. When we can practice some of these characteristics of kindness, we can be ready to offer forgiveness when needed. Ephesians 4:32

tells us to "be kind and compassionate to one another, forgiving one another, just as God also forgave you in Christ."

3. *A highly forgiving person is generous with her time, her money, and her life.*

She knows what she has is only because of what she herself has been given. This touches on similar areas as kindness, but a generous spirit goes hand in hand in with offering forgiveness. When we make it a habit to give in other ways, it's not so hard to give grace and second chances as well.

4. *A highly forgiving person lives by the Golden Rule.*

Jesus said there were two commandments that were greater than any of the others: to love God with everything we have, and to love our neighbors like we love ourselves (Mark 12:29-31). When I remember all the ways I fail God daily, and he still forgives me and gives me second chances (and third and fourth and fifth), I become greatly aware of how I need to offer that same grace to others. If I desire and yearn for grace when I find myself coming up short, how can I withhold that from others when they are in need of the same?

5. *A highly forgiving person meets with God regularly through prayer and Bible study.*

It's a sad fact that the majority of us don't read our Bibles. A poll taken by the Barna Group in 2013 found that even though 88 percent of Americans polled own a Bible, less than one in five actually read it regularly.[1] Another survey conducted by LifeWay Research reported that less than 20 percent of regular church attenders said they read their Bible daily.[2]

I haven't always done well in this area, but I've found that as with any habit, when you make time with God a priority, you can make

> When you make time with God a priority, you can make the time.

the time. Highly forgiving people know that if left to their own judgments and decisions, they wouldn't be able to offer forgiveness or let things go as easily as they can when they are spending time studying and soaking up God's truth in his Word. They apply Romans 12:2 daily: "Do not be conformed to this age, but be transformed by the renewing of your mind, so that you may discern what is the good, pleasing, and perfect will of God." We renew our minds best, we transform our hearts most readily, when we remind ourselves again and again what Scripture says and how we can live God's love out each day.

6. *A highly forgiving person offers the benefit of the doubt to others when their actions are hurtful or disappointing.*

This is a hard one for me, because my temptation is to assume the worst. When a friend doesn't call or come by as planned, instead of realizing something unexpected came up, I wonder if she just didn't care enough. If my husband forgets to help me with a project he said he would, instead of just chalking it up to an honest slip of the mind because he's busy with other things, I can quickly jump to the assumption that he intentionally lied.

By offering the benefit of the doubt to others when they do something that disappoints us, we remind ourselves that we're all human and mistakes can happen. Being willing to overlook those mistakes until we hear the whole story can help us keep relationships intact and our hearts in the right place.

> By offering the benefit of the doubt to others when they do something that disappoints us, we remind ourselves that we're all human and mistakes can happen.

7. *A highly forgiving person consistently prays for other people.*

When we pray for people, especially those who don't always rub us the right way, we're doing two things right. First, we're bringing someone else before our heavenly Father, knowing that he sees them and he knows them, and if anything is wrong, he will deal with it in his perfect way. Spending time in prayer for others also softens our hearts toward people and situations, and if our motives are right, God will often give us the insights we need.

So how did you do? Did you see any you could identify with in the list of the Highly Resentful? Could you relate to more among the Highly Forgiving? Whichever list you found yourself relating more to, know that God wants to help you develop more habits of the Highly Forgiving, and he will if you only ask. We do not have to stay where we are if we're struggling with holding on to resentment.

A Different Choice

The summer after my freshman year of college, I came home for the two-month break and volunteered to help with our church's youth choir trip. I was hungry for God's presence in my life, and I wanted to not just talk about my relationship with him but to put feet to my faith, apply it, live it out. So with this trip, I thought I'd try something. (I guess you could say this was my first experiment—I've had a few of those since then.) I knew there would be lots of opinions as there usually are with high school students—OK, with high school girls—and I figured the potential for drama could be high. So before we left, I promised God I'd stay drama free. I would help anyone I could and bless as many people as possible.

Something powerful happens when you set out each day with the intention of living it for Jesus and praying your way through it. No matter what the situation—whether a van broke down or sound equipment didn't work correctly or someone started complaining, threatening to influence the mood of everyone around them—I felt peace.

I felt joy, too, and I knew it didn't come from what I did or didn't do but from God working through me. Others noticed too.

We were standing in line for something, waiting, and a girl next to me, probably fifteen or sixteen years old, sighed loudly and pushed her sweaty bangs out of her face. She turned to face me and looked me up and down with a curious expression. "Sara, you have been upbeat and positive this entire trip—you haven't seemed to let anything get to you. Why?"

"I don't know," I said with a smile. "God is just really good."

He was. God blessed me through that trip, and I felt a physical and emotional difference in me and in how I related to others. But before you roll your eyes, set this book aside, and cast me into the "so heavenly minded she's no earthly good" category, let me explain why I share that story with you.

First, keep in mind we were on a mission trip—we were singing songs about Jesus and sharing him with people we met along the way. There have been plenty of moments since that trip I haven't felt so joyful or peaceful. Neither have the people who live with me.

If you've ever been on a mission trip, you know how much fun it is to be on that spiritual mountaintop with God, getting the opportunity to have your full and undivided attention on what he's placed before you to do. But eventually every mountain climber must come down.

Just as Moses had to leave his Ten Commandments experience with God and come back to the reality of the selfish, spoiled brats he was leading (who, while he was gone, had decided to throw a party and throw everything God had told them out the window), a Christ-follower at some point has to come back from their mountaintop experience to their reality known as life. We're talking bills and chores and cars that break down and kids who throw up and, yes, friends and family who don't always act like we wish they would. The joy and the peace and the patience and the kindness don't always seep as easily from

> If I can intentionally give Jesus my days in any given week, I can be intentional with giving him every day of my life.

every pore of your body—sometimes you may wonder if those virtues are there at all.

I share that story with you because of what that experience taught me. If I can intentionally give Jesus my days in any given week, I can be intentional with giving him every day of my life. I can be deliberate about giving him the relationships in my life, even the hard ones...*especially* the hard ones.

We can let go of slights and offenses before they take hold and before they grow into that white noise that's harder to clear out of our heads. But this isn't easy or as simple as it sounds. Our natural tendency isn't to let go but to hold on for dear life—to hold on to our rights and our privileges because if we don't, something may change and we may not like it.

Just look at how easy we get offended today. If one person finds a Christmas program at their child's school offensive because they don't believe in Christ and don't want to hear songs about Christ, the entire performance gets scrubbed of religious meaning. Someone can be sued for praying in a public venue because another person doesn't like it.

But being offended isn't reserved for just the non-Christians. Christians have gotten pretty good at it too. We've found things in our churches to be offended about for years. I heard once from a pastor whose church was about to split over four old church pews. The sanctuary was cramped and it was hard for people to slide in and out, and so the pastor wanted to remove four pews to make seating more comfortable. But because someone's granny bought those pews for the church fifty years before, lines were drawn and a battle began.

We get mad at people outside our churches too. We're offended when celebrities say ungodly things at award shows, or when our favorite chicken sandwich chain gets boycotted because they don't support a lifestyle the world says is OK, or when our favorite duck-hunter, reality-television family gets dropped from their mainstream cable network for quoting Scripture. So we get offended, we get angry, and we go to battle, arguing online with people who don't know Jesus, don't share our beliefs, and don't understand the Bible. Instead of sounding like love, we sound exactly like they do. We call them names, we call them stupid, and we moan out loud why so many people hate Jesus.

At Christmastime, we get angry when the local big-box store employee, following her company's policy, tells us "Happy Holidays" as we exit the checkout line, and we snap back, "Merry *Christ*mas!" sounding more like Ebenezer Scrooge (before his three visitors) than Christ. If you want to say "Merry Christmas," say it, but don't shoot the other guy as you do it. (Sort of negates the whole Christmas spirit thing, don't you think?)

I still remember not too long ago when an atheist family backed by a humanist organization asked the Supreme Court to remove "under God" from the Pledge of Allegiance because it was offensive for Americans who didn't believe in God. Christians were incensed, and for months you couldn't go to a sporting event or a public gathering where you didn't hear the words "UNDER GOD!" screamed loud and proud whenever the pledge was said (and I do mean screamed). Too bad we just sounded angry when we did it. But we were offended and we were fighting back.

I'm just not sure it's our right to fight—or at least fight in that way. Are the battles we choose the battles God's chosen for us?

You may be reading this, thinking, *But Sara, I haven't done any of those things. I don't argue with people online, and I don't snap at poor cashiers at Christmastime.* I don't, either— but other Christians do, and we're seen as all the same. You may not make your offenses known in public ways, but passive aggressiveness can be an art, especially among women and particularly those

> Our biggest offenses start with each other, with the people around us who live in our homes.

of us in the South. Have you ever heard a southern woman say, "Bless her heart!"? She's not really blessing her. She's really saying, "What an idiot!"

Truth.

So we focus on these battles that grab our attention—in the media or on Facebook or Twitter with hashtags that plant our flags and announce our teams. But the battle we really should focus on is the battle within ourselves. Here's why: Our biggest offenses don't start with national news or politically correct trends or what Hollywood is or isn't doing to promote Christian values. Our biggest offenses start with each other, with the people around us who live in our homes and visit in our living rooms and meet us around dining room tables on holidays and call or don't call us depending on the day and the mood. That's our battle, and that's a battle I'm praying God wins for you and for me both.

Paul writes about this battle of our hearts and minds in the seventh chapter of Romans. Our problem is sin. Even if we know Christ, we still battle sin. You're not immune to sin just because you prayed the prayer and made a promise. My belief is that you become a bigger target because God's enemy is now your enemy, too, and he (the enemy) knows it.

Paul explains it this way: "For I know that nothing good lives in me, that is, in my flesh. For the desire to do what is good is with me, but there is no ability to do it" (Romans 7:18). Even though we may desire to do God's will, our human nature is always going to lean toward sin. Only through God's power and work in our lives can we correct our course and choose God's better way. The Greek word for flesh is *sarx*; it stresses how ineffective our human efforts are when it comes to spiritual matters. We can't rise above sin on our own.

The good news is that Jesus didn't die on a cross so we could be offended. He died so that he could come back—and we could know grace. He died and came back so we could see what true forgiveness looked like in human form.

What Happens When We Say No to Resentment

As I looked through my Bible and found so many examples of different individuals who got offended and upset or just ticked off, either with God or with other people, I was a little surprised. The list goes on and on. The good news is we're not alone in our grudges. The bad news is, by the evidence, grudges and resentment are really easy to grow. Here are just a few examples.

> The good news is we're not alone in our grudges.

Esau had a grudge against his brother, Jacob, when Jacob stole his birthright and blessing (Genesis 27:41). Saul resented David's clear anointing by God to take his place as king and was so jealous of David's success and accomplishments that he tried to kill him (1 Samuel 18:7-11). When King Herod married Herodias, his brother Philip's wife, John the Baptist spoke out against the union, telling Herod the marriage was not a marriage in God's eyes. Herodias was furious. In her resentment, she waited for the right opportunity and when it came, she had John executed (Mark 6:14-29).

But if there's one story in the Bible (maybe besides Jesus and his crucifixion) where we might see resentment as a feeling rightly and well-deserved, it would be Joseph's in Genesis 37 and following. This guy couldn't catch a break. First, his jealous brothers dumped him in a hole and sold him to slave traders who hauled him off to Egypt, while his brothers told his father he was dead. Then the slave traders sold Joseph to an official in Pharaoh's court, where he excelled in his job overseeing the official's household until the man's wife made a pass at him, and when he did the right thing and resisted, she lied about him, and the official had him hauled off to prison. In prison, Joseph still saw success in what he was asked to do, even going out of his way to help other prisoners, but at a moment when it most counted, he was forgotten…for years.

If I put myself in Joseph's place, I'm not sure I could have kept going like he did, with a good attitude, always looking for how I could help, always being available for God to use me, no matter where I ended up. I'm pretty sure I wouldn't have just run away from that woman, but I might have kept running, out the door and out of the city and out into the desert, hiding under a cactus somewhere, complaining to God and asking why he cared so little about me to do me this way.

> Would God still have rewarded Joseph had he held a grudge?

But Joseph didn't do that. He also didn't stay in prison.

Over and over we're told that "the LORD was with Joseph," and he gave him success. He extended kindness to him. He offered him favor. I'm not sure God would have given him the same blessings if Joseph had held on to resentment toward his brothers for what they'd done. Would God still have rewarded Joseph had he held a grudge against them? If he'd stayed awake at night in his bed, replaying the scene over and over again where they threw him into the ground and dreaming about what he would do if he ever saw them again? The heartache and misery he might return? If he had let bitterness take root in his heart so that everywhere he went, he saw the faces of his brothers laughing, with no compassion, with no concern, and if he'd thought of revenge or payback…would God still have been with Joseph?

If you've read Joseph's story, you know how it ends. You know he goes on to be appointed Pharaoh's right-hand man, and that he lives out a rags-to-riches tale of a young man once a slave who's now the governor. You also know he's not just the governor, but the man solely responsible for saving Egypt, including the people who lived in its surrounding lands (as well as Joseph's family), from seven years of hardship and famine. So while it's tempting with Joseph's story to see it as only about God's purpose for our lives, or as just an example of God's plan versus our own, or simply as a story of our calling versus our comfort—we don't want to do that.

We don't want to see his story in only one of those ways, because we'll miss one of the greatest truths about his story. If you read the last scene in Genesis 45 of Joseph's time with his brothers in the royal palace—after he's put them through their paces, after he's made them sweat the small stuff, after he's confused their plans and turned things completely upside down for them (which I don't think was his way of revenge but a way of testing their hearts to see if and how much they'd changed)—Joseph doesn't reveal himself to be the brother who still got everything he wanted. He doesn't laugh in their faces and say, "How's it feel to be on the other side now, bros?" He doesn't scorn them or threaten them.

Instead, he faces them and he cries. Hard. He sobs so intensely that for a minute no sound can come out and he hunches over just to grab a breath. He bawls like a baby, as we in the South like to say. This strong, successful national leader weeps so loudly that everyone in the house can hear it.

That sweet, heartbreaking sound of forgiveness, that cry of grace and reconciliation and humility and love all rolled into one, echoes through the walls and through the courtyards and into the hearts of his brothers, who didn't deserve his forgiveness though they desperately needed it.

That day, when Joseph faced the men responsible for taking him away from his beloved father, the men who sent him away from everything he'd held familiar, I don't believe that was the first day Joseph forgave them. I think that day was simply the culmination, the final gift of forgiveness he'd already given years and years before.

> I don't believe that was the first day Joseph forgave them. I think that day was simply the culmination.

Maybe he didn't do it when he was sitting there in the pit his brothers threw him in, but he could have done it on his journey to Egypt. I think early on, Joseph made a choice to trust God more than man, and to let God take care of the battles that mattered, and Joseph would leave the rest alone.

He tells his brothers not to be worried or angry or feel guilty, because "God sent me ahead of you to preserve life…God sent me ahead of you to establish you as a remnant within the land and to keep you alive by a great deliverance. Therefore it was not you who sent me here, but God" (Genesis 45:5-8).

We cannot see God's plan when we can see only our pain. Joseph saw God's plan because he chose to let go of the difficult circumstances that brought him to Egypt, and he grabbed on and trusted God with everything he had.

> We cannot see God's plan when we can see only our pain.

Maybe that's a big part of all this offensiveness business. These grudge matches we play. We don't worry so much about what offends us, what little slights or hurtful words bother us, when we worry more about what God wants with us and how he wants to use us.

I read something by Oswald Chambers that made me think more about this idea of my will versus God's will, and how it's such a big part of offering or receiving forgiveness. When we look at this idea of letting go of things that hurt us—whether minor abrasions at the surface of our hearts or very deep wounds with thick scars—we are faced with a choice: our will or God's. Chambers talks about being ready "to be offered," offered to God for him to do whatever he wants with us.

> "I am now ready to be offered." It is a transaction of will, not of sentiment. *Tell* God you are ready to be offered; then let the consequences be what they may, there is no strand of complaint now, no matter what God chooses. God puts you through the crisis in private, no one person can help another. Externally the life may be the same, *the difference is in will* [emphasis mine]. Go through the crisis in will, then when it comes externally there will be no thought of the cost.[3]

Would we be less likely to find resentment in life if we were waking up each day "ready to be offered"? Chambers goes on to paint a picture of offering ourselves on the altar, which "means fire—burning and purification and insulation for one purpose only, the destruction of every affinity that God has not started and of every attachment that is not an attachment in God. *You do not destroy it, God does*...After this way of fire, there is nothing that oppresses or depresses. When the crisis arises, you realize that *things cannot touch you as they used to do.*"

Wow. Aren't those powerful words? They can speak into our hearts when it comes to holding grudges or withholding forgiveness.

Things cannot touch you as they used to do.

Believe it. Trust God has you in his hand and he is with you. Choose to practice habits of forgiveness instead of habits of resentment. Let go of those little hurts, the ones that distract you like the loud ticking of a clock in an otherwise quiet room, or the ones that grate against your spirit like sounds of fingernails on a chalkboard. Let them go. He's never intended you to hold on to them in the first place.

> Choose to practice habits of forgiveness instead of habits of resentment.

"Therefore, God's chosen ones, holy and loved, put on heartfelt compassion, kindness, humility, gentleness, and patience, accepting one another and forgiving one another if anyone has a complaint against another. Just as the Lord has forgiven you, so you must also forgive" (Colossians 3:12-13).

Five Ways to Choose Forgiveness
over Resentment Right Now

1. **Offer compassion.** When someone says something unkind or thoughtless, refuse to take it personally. Instead, reflect compassion, a characteristic of Christ himself. When someone is rude or abrupt, there's usually something else going on behind the tough or ugly attitude. You never know what kind of day someone has already had before they get to you. But there is always a possibility you can help make it better.

2. **Offer kindness.** Christ was kind in his dealings with everyday people like you and me. Is there a coworker who seems to be on a mission to rub you the wrong way? Offer to buy her lunch one day. Is there another mom who drives you crazy with her constant conversation of how perfect her children are? Be friendly toward her anyway, and give her a smile when you see her, instead of running the other way. We're reminded in Jeremiah that the heart is "a puzzle that no one can figure out," but God gets to the root of the problem and treats us as we "really are, not as [we] pretend to be" (Jeremiah 17:9-10 MSG).

3. **Offer humility.** "The humble will have joy after joy in the LORD" (Isaiah 29:19). Being real with people goes a long way toward building authentic relationships. Being real with yourself goes a long way in growing your relationship with God closer.

   When we are willing to show only our best or, even worse, constantly bragging about our best, whether on social media or in line at the grocery store, we're opening the door for others to be resentful toward us and make us look like the jerk no one wants to hang out with.

Humble brags don't count, either. You know, the little statements people make like "I'm so tired from trying to keep my six-bedroom house clean," or "Wow, we haven't been home one night this week for dinner, but I guess I should be glad my daughter is on track to make the Olympics in eight years with all the gymnastics classes her coach wants her to do!" Yeah. Someone very wise told me once it's better to say nothing and let others talk about your accomplishments, because they will talk about what is really worthy of mention. There is important truth in that.

4. **Offer gentleness.** As I get older, and I meet and hear from so many different women in different seasons of life with such a variety of experiences—both good and bad—I am increasingly aware of the frailty and the brokenness a lot of us hide daily. Proverbs reminds us that a "gentle answer turns away anger, but a harsh word stirs up wrath" (Proverbs 15:1). I've got to admit, though, my first reaction in a lot of cases isn't always to be gentle—especially when it involves my husband or my son! I can lose patience with women too. But working in women's ministry for the last seven years and with a team of women's leaders who all have their own stuff happening within their families and their lives has taught me to be more gentle, more understanding, and to realize that I don't always know the whole story. When we choose to be gentle, it's easier to be forgiving too.

5. **Offer patience.** I think patience goes hand in hand with forgiveness (maybe that's why both can be so hard). When we're willing to wait on an outcome or for someone to do something they've promised, we're applying self-control and compassion at the same time and really, that's part of what forgiveness is about. We read in Proverbs 19:11 that "a person's insight gives him patience, and his virtue is to overlook an

offense." That means when our heart is more patient, our actions are more forgiving.

So practice patience with the car in front of you that's driving 25 miles an hour in a 35 mph zone. Practice patience when your child takes forever with their homework or keeps forgetting to close the door to his room so Shredder the dog doesn't get in there and eat something else. (Glasses, maybe?) But be careful about praying for patience. I've done that a couple times and a word to the wise: God is very good at helping you with that.

3

In Seasons of Rumble

If you don't like the weather right now, just wait a few minutes and it will change." We like to say that here in Louisiana, but I'm pretty sure other states have tried to make the same claim.

During the summer, rain showers can happen for a few minutes every day sometimes. I remember the first summer after we moved back here how much I enjoyed those mini cloudbursts, so much so that I would go stand outside under the porch and breathe in the dampness. I loved those random showers because for just a little while after the raindrops stopped, the temps lowered, and all the dust and the lovebug carcasses splattered across car windshields got washed away.

Rainstorms are a different story. They often happen when the humidity is already thick and my hair refuses to cooperate. The rumbling of thunder miles away can go on and on for so long, you start to wonder if a train track got moved next to your house in the middle of the night.

Do you know the sound I'm talking about? I'm not talking about thunderclaps or loud booms or sharp cracks or big giant chambers of sound that mimic what transformers sound like exploding. This sound is more subdued, but you definitely know it's there. For stretches of time, you hear this constant low-pitched rumble, this growl that you might mistake coming from your stomach if you knew it wasn't coming from outside. Again and again, the sound turns over, like rocks in a tumbler, and there's no letting up. It just keeps going with no sign of when it will stop.

The first couple of times I heard those rumbles, I thought of a ship's hull scraping rocks. I could imagine being in that thing, trying to walk upright, even while that raspy, grating noise groans all around you and the tremors from it are underneath your feet, keeping you leaning to one side, awkwardly, just trying not to fall down.

But when the sound does stop, when the thunder mercifully quits for a moment, the immediate quiet cuts in loudly, and all that seems to ring in my ears for one brief, peaceful moment is relief. With the exception of the faintest tapping of raindrops dancing on my roof, the sound of sweet, sweet silence restores my senses, and I feel upright once again. I can stand once more.

> We are physically uncomfortable, and we have no idea when the rumble will stop.

Some events in our lives feel like that ongoing thunderous rumble. We are physically uncomfortable, and we have no idea when the rumble will stop or when the relief of sweet silence will come. So we hide in our houses or hide in our choices or try to distract ourselves from the noise with other things, like other noises to drown out the uncomfortable growl always rolling around out there in the distance, always *grrring* for our attention.

I've had seasons of my life where I've lived with the thunderous rumble. Where the hurt was always there when I woke up and when I went to sleep, and I was always uncomfortable and frustrated and out of sorts because I had no idea how to let the pain go. Some of those stories I can share and some stories I can't, because they're not only mine to tell. But I hope the lessons I've learned from all my seasons of rumble can help you learn to cope through yours.

I think it's safe to say I grew up in a loving home but a home with a lot of problems. Most families come with problems, and none of us really have a say in which problems we get, only how we deal with them and what we learn to do and not do with our own families as time goes by and we all get a little older. I just don't ever remember a time where I thought my parents' marriage was a close one. There are a lot of reasons for that, but I know both my mother and father did the best they could, and they never went into their marriage with divorce as an option.

Twenty-nine years later, though, divorce became their end result.

The year they separated was the year our son, Caleb, was born. Cliff and I were in Tennessee at the time, living in a little apartment off the university campus where I worked and we both attended classes. My mom and dad brought my younger brother and sister to see their new nephew, and despite still being sleep-deprived, I noticed a little more tension between them. Granted, there was always some tension going on between them, but this time, there also seemed to be more sadness in their faces. Weariness.

A few months later my dad took a contract job in another state, something he'd done for a few years, but this time was different. This time, my parents told us, he wouldn't come back. Their marriage was over.

Growing up, I don't remember having a lot of friends whose parents were divorced. But I have a lot of friends now whose parents are. I'm not sure if it's any better being an adult child of divorce than it is when you're younger. Maybe as an adult, you understand more; at least you're old enough to have an idea of what the problems were and where the conflicts couldn't get resolved.

> I'm not sure if it's any better being an adult child of divorce than it is when you're younger.

There's a sense of emptiness that stays with you, though, a loss you just don't get over the next day. This isn't a little thing like someone cutting you off in traffic or someone at church asking if you're pregnant (and you aren't, and you have no plans to be, and you *thought* the shirt you chose that morning looked good on you). No, when you're dealing with something as painful as a divorce, whether it's your parents or your own or that of a close friend or family member, there isn't a Band-Aid big enough to make the hurt all go away quickly.

These are Big Hurts. Big Hurts are complicated. Big Hurts sometimes take lots of time to heal, and forgiveness for Big Hurts can take longer than you might want or expect.

I'm not proud of this fact, but for almost two years following their divorce, I didn't speak to my dad. I didn't talk to my mom very often either. When we did talk, there was usually tension on my part. Since we lived over nine hours away, it wasn't hard to play the avoid game. I blamed it on being busy; I was a young wife with a new baby, trying to juggle family and school and career and ambitions.

I said I was busy, but the truth is I was just really bitter.

I said I was busy, but the truth is I was just really bitter. I wasn't thinking about my parents' pain and what they were going through, saying good-bye to a relationship that had lasted for almost three decades. I wasn't thinking about how both of them were suddenly forced to start over, how they had to once again learn to be on their own, by themselves, solely responsible for every decision they each made, and figuring out what that meant and what that looked like. I didn't think about them very much, if I'm honest. I just thought about my own pain and how at a time in my life when I'd wanted the stability of my parents the most, it wasn't there.

That white noise of bitterness stayed with me for a few years. Judgmental whispers were always in the back of my mind. *If they'd just tried a little harder*, or *if just one of them had tried a little harder, cared a little more*, maybe they would have stayed together. If *their* parents had tried a little harder, loved a little more, cared enough, done more to stop a negative cycle from even starting. Family get-togethers wouldn't be so difficult or awkward or uncomfortable. Schedules wouldn't be so complicated. Most married couples have to deal with at least two families around the holidays, but to juggle three? Both of my parents stayed single, and because I was the oldest, I felt responsible for their singleness. I stressed about Christmas holidays and birthdays, knowing I needed to make sure they were taken care of with gifts, with people in their lives, but not really feeling very giving at all.

The noise in my head and my heart wouldn't quit, and I wasn't nice to be around for anyone. I could be grumpy and cynical and sarcastic, and I didn't fully trust anyone except myself. My parents' divorce only reinforced my opinion that relationships were too messy and not worth making the time.

Bitterness does that to you. When life happens and circumstances feel unfair, when you sense yourself in the crosshairs of an undeserved target, or maybe just as an innocent bystander not looking for trouble or for problems, you can quickly move from sadness to resentment, from denial to anger. You might get mad at other people, putting blame squarely on their shoulders, or you might even get mad at God.

The thing about bitterness, though, is it's not easy to hide. Eventually, you expose yourself. Your sour feelings come out.

Naomi was bitter. After escaping a famine in Bethlehem by moving to Moab with her husband and sons, in a period of about ten years, she lost not only her husband but both sons too. We read Naomi's story in the book of Ruth. She was despondent. She was heartbroken. Nothing Naomi saw in front of her could make her life better. She believed God hated her and had nothing left for her. Even when her daughter-in-law Ruth refused to leave her side and stayed with her on the journey back to Bethlehem, Naomi was so consumed with bitterness, she insisted on changing her name to Mara, which means "bitter."

> How easily we can be changed by our circumstances and challenges, by the Big Hurts we come up against.

I think it's interesting the name Naomi means "pleasant." How easily we can be changed by our circumstances and challenges, by the Big Hurts we come up against. Naomi went from feeling joy and happiness and satisfaction to reeling from great hopelessness, unhappiness, and great dissatisfaction. She couldn't initially see the gift God gave her in Ruth, but she would.

I can relate to feelings of unhappiness and dissatisfaction because ignoring what's causing your bitterness offers only a temporary fix. Eventually, you have enough of the constant rumble in your ears and you start to realize something has to change.

For me, that point of change happened on a work assignment at a retreat center tucked away in the mountains of North Carolina. There were two back-to-back weeklong events I had to cover for my office, which meant that in between those events, I had a free day over the weekend. The good thing about being away is you don't have a lot of distractions or noise to pull your attention. The hard thing about being away is that whatever is weighing on your heart at the time comes quickly to the surface when there's nothing else to push it down.

> The hard feelings I'd carried around for so long had worn me down and weighed me down.

I was drained. The hard feelings I'd carried around for so long had worn me down and weighed me down. I threw my Bible in my backpack and headed out into the sunshine, with the thought I might hike a little way up a nearby path and spend some needed time with God. The day was beautiful, the air warm but dry, a soft cool breeze blew occasionally through the trees. I tried to breathe in and relax a little as I took my time hiking up the dirt path, keeping an eye out for markers and some sense of where I was going.

Truth: I'm not very good with direction. If I were your GPS, and you wanted to go to Florida, you'd probably end up in Oklahoma. I think the politically correct term is directionally challenged (like vertically challenged for short people). My husband doesn't understand how I can be so bad with directions. But he was a Boy Scout and learned how to use a compass, and there's that whole Navy Seabee thing for seventeen years. He's had a few opportunities to learn how to find his way around.

As I moved up the path, my eyes kept looking up at the enormous trees that stood so tall and grand against the deep blue background of the sky. I veered with the dirt path to the right past a few more trees and came into an odd clearing of sorts surrounded by—yes, more trees.

This wasn't right. I looked directly behind me at the dirt that *looked* like the path I had been on. But there was no more path from where I was standing. I turned around again. Was that the way I came? All of the trees suddenly looked exactly alike. And I'd left my bread crumbs at home. Whoops.

Seriously. Two minutes on this hike and I was already lost? I smiled first and then just laughed out loud. I couldn't help it. Here I was, standing at the *beginning* of a mountain, surrounded by nature, lost as a goose. Someone had even warned me before I left the lodge to make sure I didn't get lost, since there were frequent bear sightings, and here I was, fulfilling their prophecy before I'd ever had a chance to break a sweat or take a drink from my water bottle.

I quickly whispered a little prayer to God, something along the lines of "A little help here, please?" That's when I heard voices, coming from somewhere down the path. I walked a few feet back where I'd been, trying to make out the group I could hear coming from the same direction I had, and trying not to look like I was lost.

A family emerged from the trees, parents and an older son, and as they got closer, I did the first thing I thought of: I bent down to tie my already tied shoe. The woman smiled and threw a little wave at me and a "Beautiful day, huh?" as they hiked on by, and I smiled and said "Yeah! Great!" with a whole lot more enthusiasm than I probably needed to. I slowly stood back up, casually pulled on my backpack, and walked behind them, maintaining a respectable distance but still with them in sight at least long enough until I found a spot where I wanted to sit.

Twenty minutes later, and much farther up the mountain, I found a nice flat piece of rock that overlooked a clearing below. I sat down with my Bible on my lap and took in the beautiful view as I thought about why I was up there.

> I'd reached in and had held on to something I shouldn't have picked up. I'd refused to let go.

I was tired of feeling the opposite of what I was looking at, there among the beauty of God's creation. I didn't feel beautiful, I felt ugly, and I knew the attitudes I'd let take root in my heart had also taken over my life. The bitter feelings I'd let form about my parents' divorce had affected my outlook on other things too. I knew change was needed. I knew a *heart* change was needed, and only God could help me do that. Forgiveness was needed, and not really because my parents needed to apologize, but because of the hard feelings I'd formed. I'd reached in and had held on to something I shouldn't have picked up. I'd refused to let go.

I pulled out my Bible, flipped to the concordance, and found a section on bitterness and read through some of the passages listed there. Hebrews 12:15 pointed out that we should be on the lookout for bitterness, so "that no one falls short of the grace of God and that no root of bitterness springs up, causing trouble and by it, defiling many." And then I read Genesis 12.

Abraham had just come out of Egypt, where he'd lived due to a famine that was happening where he had been. A lot had gone wrong in Egypt for Abraham—he'd lied to Pharaoh about Sarah being his sister and not his wife, and because of that, God had brought disease to Pharaoh's house until the truth was revealed and Abraham and his wife and all his belongings and livestock and flocks were sent away.

In Genesis 13, Abraham and Sarah were now living with his nephew Lot. But Abraham still had problems. The land where all of them were living had limited resources and couldn't sustain both Abraham's animals and Lot's. Fighting had broken out between their herdsmen, and probably even between Abraham and Lot as they tried to manage the conflict. Something had to give.

"Please," Abraham told Lot, "let's not have quarreling between you and me." Then he gave his nephew the choice of which land he wanted.

As I read Abraham's story, I saw the traits I needed to have in my life and the attitude I needed toward my parents. In Egypt he had been selfish and guilty of thinking more of himself than anyone else (he had told Pharaoh his wife was his sister because he feared for his own life), and the consequences of those actions taught him how to deal with future conflict in a different way. He could have continued to be selfish in the problems he faced with Lot, but instead he chose generosity and selflessness. *He let any concern for himself go. He trusted God to take care of him.*

So Lot chose the better land for his animals and family, and Abraham was left with the lesser of the two. But I believe God used that situation to test Abraham and to see if he really had learned anything from his experience in Egypt, and as a result, God blessed him by promising him that he would have the land he saw. God promised he would make Abraham's "offspring like the dust of the earth" (Genesis 13:16), his

> I knew it was time to trust God for the future and stop holding on to the past.

descendants many, his legacy great. In response, Abraham built an altar to God, signifying and remembering what God would do.

I sat there for a long time, praying quietly, tears flowing, as I poured out my hurts to God there on that little patch of mountain. I knew it was time to let those feelings of bitterness go. I knew it was time to trust God for the future and stop holding on to the past. It wouldn't be easy, but it was important.

Finding two small rocks nearby and a Sharpie in my backpack, I wrote on one rock "Mom" and on the other rock "Dad," and I prayed then and there that God would restore my love for them, that he would help take away the hard feelings and that I could leave those feelings there with those rocks on that mountain so I could keep moving forward, looking for both the blessings God had for me and for my parents.

I thought about my experience with getting lost earlier and how it took a voice to help me find my way back to where I needed to be. Only when I listen for God's voice can I find relief from things that hold me back from forgiving or even from giving. I have to be willing to trust God enough to surrender my will for his when it comes to the relationships in my life.

> I felt free and I felt whole once again. The bitterness was gone.

This isn't easy. I can't say that the relationships with my parents are perfect today, but I can say God has done a lot in all of us, and he has continued to work on my heart over the years. When I made my way back from that hike, the first thing I did was call both my parents, one at a time, and apologize for my attitude and how I'd treated them. I felt free and I felt whole once again. The bitterness was gone.

Though little moments of hurt still crop up (like around the holidays when I'm trying to please everyone and feeling like I'm doing the exact opposite), and I have to catch myself and give it all back to God, I know it was on that mountain, away from the rumbles, that the healing began.

Where Big Hurts Go

For years, before I knew her, a friend of mine prayed for the opportunity to be a mom. Eventually, she and her husband felt led to international adoption, and they were so excited when they got the news they would be parents of a precious little boy from Russia, the son they had prayed for and dreamed about for so long.

But just a couple of years after their son came into their lives, they began noticing things that were different from other children. Their beautiful boy, the one they'd looked forward to loving on and being with, watching him play baseball at the local youth park and throwing balls around with his dad in their backyard, the son they couldn't wait to see what God would do with—maybe a teacher, or a doctor, or a pastor—was diagnosed with a severe form of autism. As they researched the diagnosis, they realized the weight of the realities they faced. Their little boy wouldn't grow up to be a teacher or a doctor. He would never go to college. He would never be able to really care for himself. He would always depend on them or others for his care.

Sixteen years later, I watch my friend and I can't imagine the disappointment and the heartache she felt hearing that diagnosis. Thinking about all of those dreams that had to change. All of those desires she'd had that got traded in for God's desires for her son, simpler goals and dreams. Like curling up with him at home and watching his favorite Barney video when he's not feeling well. Her son is still precious to her, but he's now a bigger, more unwieldy teenager who is harder to control when he has outbursts or gets upset. I know she prays for more good days in a week than bad days. Bad days are the hard days, and the hard days are when she prays the hardest.

> Though the diagnosis of her son caused a big hurt, she has recognized with time that she serves an even bigger God.

But here is what I know about my friend. Though the diagnosis of her son caused a big hurt, she has recognized with time that she serves an even bigger God. Her son's condition hasn't slowed her down. She hasn't hid from the world or hid her son away from the world. She takes one day at a time, and she serves wherever God opens a door, seeing and sharing God's beautiful blessings despite the storms life brings. People watch her and her husband and their family—their older son, as well as their youngest son who was born to them, healthy and smart, several years after their first son's adoption. This is a family with an amazing testimony of God's grace and strength. We're reminded by their story that God's plans aren't always our own, but his plans are always best.

That last statement may be one of truth, but it isn't one that rolls off our tongues, not without a little wincing in our hearts, maybe. Not when the hurt is still fresh; sometimes, not even when the hurt happened years ago. When someone very close to you dies, and a well-meaning friend tells you, "God just needed him more" (as someone recently told a friend who lost her father to a heart attack), your initial response might not be to agree. You did need him. You needed him in your life. You loved him and you needed his encouragement and reminders that everything would be OK when things got tough. You needed the laughter he brought and the tears he helped wipe away. It might not have been God's plan, but it was your plan, and it was a plan you really needed to happen. But the plan didn't, and now you're left to bury a father before he should have gone.

Or maybe God's plan was for you to lose your job, and that really wasn't in your plan, and the fear that now weighs on you about what you're going to do for income and how you're going to pay your bills competes with the hurt you're feeling that your boss or your team or your company didn't want you, they didn't need you, they didn't see the importance you brought each and every day to that job you loved. And so you wonder, after you tuck the kids into bed and start perusing all the job sites online, what is God's plan, anyway? Why couldn't it have been your plan?

So all of us deal with Big Hurts. But God *is* bigger than those hurts, and stronger, and able to take your hurt and do something beautiful with it.

He heals.

No, this doesn't mean he brings your loved one back from the dead or restores your job or heals your child or restores your marriage or your parents' marriage or all the other ways we ask—no, we beg—for him to intercede for us.

He doesn't heal our circumstances for circumstances' sake.

He heals our hearts, for his sake.

> He doesn't heal our circumstances for circumstances' sake. He heals our hearts, for his sake.

He reminds us that he wants us in a constant state of dependence on him, so we learn that the brokenness and Big Hurts and painful situations we encounter are not the time to declare our independence from God— but to *declare*, through tears, through wails, through heartbreak and suffering, even through clenched teeth sometimes, our *dependence* on God and our understanding that no matter what he's walking us through, that he's walking us *through*.

So we don't have to be bitter. We don't have to put up with the rumbles, the ongoing bitterness that grates just below the surface. We can give those hurts to God and then sit with eyes wide open and ears peeled, listening for his voice when the rumbles are no more, and he whispers, "Come to Me, all of you who are weary and burdened, and I will give you rest." Come, if you're broken. Come, bring your hurts. "For My yoke is easy and My burden is light" (Matthew 11:28,30).

Forgiveness happens when our hearts are fertile and available to respond to God's leading.

Five Ways to Start
Letting Go of Bitterness Right Now

1. **Tell God how you're feeling.** Sometimes bitterness grows in our hearts because we keep ignoring the hard feelings that build up and so our hurts don't go away, they just grow bigger. Make time to talk to God about how you're feeling and ask him to help you let go of the hurt. If it's a person who has hurt you, pray for that person. If it's a situation that's disappointed or upset you, ask God to show you what he wants you to learn from it. One of the verses I hold on to during hard times is Romans 8:28—"We know that *all* things work together for the good of those who love God: those who are called according to His purpose" (emphasis mine).

2. **Recognize the importance of second chances.** One of the best examples of someone holding on to bitterness in the Bible is the brother of the prodigal son. Remember that story? A man has two sons, and the youngest decides he wants to do his own thing, taking his father's inheritance and basically squandering it through irresponsible living and a party lifestyle. He comes home only after losing everything and having nowhere else to go, and his father welcomes him with big, open arms.

   The brother, however—the one who stayed and worked and did what was expected and what was right—he isn't so welcoming. Luke tells us he gets angry, unable to see past what feels so unfair (Luke 15:28-30). If you're dealing with a situation where it's hard to see past the unfairness of it all, let me encourage you to stop looking at whatever special break someone is cut or grace that is given or luck it seems the other person has received, and start counting your own blessings.

   While the brother was never thrown a welcome home

party, he also never had to experience some of the pain his kid brother put himself through. The older brother never lost the good relationship with his father, and he maintained a good reputation for himself. God offers second chances, but he also honors godly living. Never begrudge someone of that second chance, though, because you never know when you might need a second chance yourself.

3. **Admit the sin you're dealing with.** Bitterness often masks or is symptomatic of other sins in our lives, like jealousy or pride or selfishness. First John 1:8-9 reminds us, "If we say, 'We have no sin,' we are deceiving ourselves, and the truth is not in us." But "if we confess our sins, He is faithful and righteous to forgive us our sins and to cleanse us from all unrighteousness." God doesn't withhold forgiveness from us, but he can't work with a heart that's closed to him. When we can own up to what's holding us captive, whatever it is, we open the door for God to work and to change us into the women he desires us to be.

     Sometimes it's easier to write down our feelings than to say them out loud. Grab your journal or a piece of paper and write a letter to God. Be honest with what's bothering you. He already knows anyway.

4. **Stop dwelling on what happened and repeating your story.** When we've been wronged, we want everyone to know it. But the problem with repeating the cause for your bitter feelings is that it works a lot like the way a brush fire does. Brush fires start slowly, with just a little spark, but they quickly grow and gain momentum the more dry grass they find. It's tempting to talk to anyone who will listen about the horrible awful thing that's been done to us, but this is seldom a healthy approach, especially if the friends who are listening are more enablers than encouragers. They're more likely to say, "Tell

me more" and "I can't believe them," than "I know that had to hurt, but I know you can move past this."

5. **Rethink your thinking.** Bitter attitudes often come with lots of negative thoughts. Sometimes you've had these negative thoughts for so long, you don't even realize it. Philippians 4:8 gives us some great words of wisdom in reshaping and turning our thoughts toward the things God wants us to think on: "whatever is true, whatever is honorable, whatever is just, whatever is pure, whatever is lovely, whatever is commendable—if there is any moral excellence and if there is any praise—dwell on these things." Write this verse on a card and stick it on the mirror in your bathroom or on your desk at work or on the dashboard in your car. When bitterness tries to creep in, think about this verse and change your way of thinking for the better.

4

The Thing About Scars

As a kid, I was never what you might call a daredevil. Sure, I liked to play outside with my friends, ride my bike, make up games and stories, but you would never have found me hanging off a tree limb or preparing to jump off a roof like my husband tried to do as a kid before his mom mercifully stopped him. No, I was perfectly happy creating leaf houses at recess behind our elementary school (think of the layout of a house outlined in leaves—we didn't need much to keep us happy, apparently), or swinging from a rope with friends over a "creek bed" behind an empty lot in our neighborhood, which looking back, was really a very shallow drainage ditch.

Since I played it pretty safe, I didn't get hurt very often, and so I don't have that many scars. I can tell you in great detail about the ones I do have. There's the scorpion-looking one on my left knee I got when I was seven from falling on the edge of a metal table while running out to recess. It took seven stitches to close up the cut, and while we were in the waiting room at the doctor's office, I remember staring at a girl with a bloody arm whose dad said she got bit by a shark. I don't know if he was joking, but it made me think very clearly at the time that I never wanted to get bit by a shark. Still, to this day, I'll catch myself absentmindedly rubbing my scar and thinking about the girl with the shark bite.

There's the faintest pale line on my left index finger where I cut myself trying to slice apples for my brother and sister when I was maybe nine or ten years old. My mom was away and my dad, who worked shift work at the time, was sleeping. I remember I'd felt so big and older-sister-responsible until the knife I'd stuck into the apple jerked through the apple skin and stuck me instead. I panicked when I saw the blood and held my finger with a towel while I ran through the house trying to find a Band-Aid, bursting through my parents' bedroom door to look in their bathroom cabinet, until I remembered my dad was sleeping and I ran out crying. He wasn't happy about being waked so abruptly until he was alert enough to realize what happened. As he helped me treat my cut, he made me promise never to cut another apple, at least without a parent around. I'm pretty sure I kept that promise until well after college. I had a good reminder right there on my finger.

There are other scars on my knees from bike falls (I said I wasn't a daredevil; I never said I wasn't clumsy), and for a long time, I had a doozy of a scar just below my left wrist from an ironing accident (if you've read my book *My So-Called Life as a Proverbs 31 Wife*, that should make a whole lot of sense).

The thing about scars is that almost all of us who have them have stories to go with them. While I was sharing mine, you were probably thinking of your own.

But not every scar can be seen, at least not by our eyes, anyway.

I don't have a lot of those kinds of scars, but I know others who do. I have friends who grew up with scars you don't get from falling off your bike. Deep wounds that stay with you and take a really long time to heal, and even after they do, they're almost impossible to forget. Something always serves as a reminder of the story that goes with that scar, a story you don't usually want to remember. I've watched people implode, one bad decision at a time, from scars that were never

> Scars don't always cover up what hurt us in the first place.

given time to properly heal, and instead of dealing with the one scar they had, they added several more of their own doing. Scars don't always cover up what hurt us in the first place.

So when we're talking about forgiveness, we can't ignore the really hard stuff that's more difficult to forgive or let go or even think about or discuss. We're talking about scars from abuse. Something done to you by someone else, physically or emotionally, who had no business doing it. Words that were said that cut deep, like "you're stupid," or "you'll never be worth anything," or that put fear inside you, like "I'm going to beat the devil out of you." Actions that were done to you that left you feeling the same way those words made you feel.

A recent study found that one in four women and one in six men are sexually abused as children. That means in a church of two hundred members equally divided between women and men, at least forty-one people are child sexual-abuse survivors.[4] These are scars we don't talk about during Sunday school or small-group prayer request time, but they're still there, and their presence doesn't just play a part in the survivor's past, but also in that person's future.

There are other scars that stay with us, scars from the deep hurt of great loss, like the death of a child or of a spouse or a parent, and we still struggle to understand how it all makes sense. Scars from a former spouse whose choice to cheat and his last painful words to you, "I don't love you; I don't think I ever did," have made you wonder if you'll ever be able to love, or be loved, again.

If you are dealing with scars like these, let me first say I'm so sorry, friend. I'm sorry for the hurts you've received and the pain you've experienced. I'm sorry for the life experiences you've missed out on, the happiness and joy you wanted but didn't get, a feeling of wholeness that's escaped you for a long, long time. But I want you to know you aren't alone. You're not the only one who has gone through what you have, and there are others out there who understand.

I also want you to know that you don't have to deal with your hurt alone. I'm praying that as you read this book, God will give you the courage, if he hasn't already, to find an experienced, professional Christian counselor who can help you sort through your hurt and pain and find healing.

The only one who will ever fully understand our hurts is Jesus. We turn to him for help and he helps us forgive and let go. We need to let go because I don't think we realize sometimes the impact scars have on us, what those scars keep us from doing and from experiencing.

I grew up with a deep craving for approval from anyone who would give it, and that feeling didn't change when I hit the workforce. I didn't want to just do my best; I wanted to *be* the best, and my 100 mph approach to everything reflected that. Impressing my boss and my coworkers meant more to me than anything, and because of that, anything less than "you're amazing" left me feeling dissatisfied and in a funk.

> I didn't want to just do my best; I wanted to *be* the best.

If I got negative feedback, I could be down in the dumps for weeks. I remember the notes I sometimes got from a former boss who liked to outline in handwritten detail things I'd missed or ways I'd disappointed him; they could leave me sobbing in a coworker's office, crying my eyes out, wondering where I'd gone wrong.

So I was nervous when the time came to sit down for my first job evaluation with a new boss. I'd worked for this Christian publishing company for just under a year, in a job that I loved. I got to write, to see my work published, to travel occasionally, and I was excited about the projects I was involved with and the contributions I was making. In that first year I was there, I'd traveled overseas twice to write stories of faith during the Iraq war, which turned into a book I did with a high-profile author later that year. Though I knew being a young rookie writer with a book deal didn't make me very popular with the more seasoned writers in the office, I couldn't hold back my excitement in everything God seemed to be doing in my life, and I just assumed they'd be excited too. I worked hard in my job, writing as many stories as I could and eagerly soaking up everything I could learn from the others.

My boss had come to his new position from working in public relations for a significantly large retailer. He was a reserved man who thought before he spoke, but was straight with you when he did. As we sat in the corporate café area at a little table sipping coffee, he informed me it was his practice when doing evaluations to offer not just his thoughts, but also what he called a 360-degree review. He liked to give coworkers and others who interacted with an employee the chance to respond, anonymously, with their feedback of that person's work.

You probably already can guess where this is headed. So let me just interrupt for a moment and ask, "Who uses anonymous job evaluations by coworkers up for the *same* available money in raises and the *same* levels of promotion and advancement without figuratively putting a 'kick me up one side and down the other' sign on the poor employee sitting in front of you?" Wow, that felt good. I think a breakthrough was just made. Moving on.

The comments he shared from my coworkers were anything but good. "She's not a good writer." "She's self-centered." "She isn't a team player." "She has a lot to learn."

> My wings got clipped that day and left a painful scar on my heart. But the message was received.

As I sat there, listening to him read their painful words as if he were reading the news from his morning paper, I felt my heart and my spirit completely wilt. I didn't understand. I was all for constructive criticism—tell me what I'm not doing well and how I can improve—but these comments all felt a lot more personal than professional. I went home that night and cried on my husband's shoulder. My wings got clipped that day and left a painful scar on my heart. But the message was received.

I no longer talked in the office about anything except the projects at hand. When my book released just a couple of months following my evaluation, I kept my comments and excitement to a minimum, even though the company I worked for was the one who published it. I didn't say a word to anyone when the publisher offered me another book deal. I kept my head down, I did my job, and I licked my wound and waited for the hurt to heal.

Something inside me had changed, and for me, not for the better.

After another year passed, I went through my annual evaluation again, and this time, those anonymous 360-degree reviews were glowing. But I didn't leave that meeting with my boss that day feeling any more happy or carefree or satisfied than the year before. I knew that the real difference for the evaluations was because something inside me had changed, and for me, not for the better. Six months later I turned in my notice.

The thing about a scar is that even if you change your environment or your situation or your circumstances, you still may feel what you felt when you first received it. The scar doesn't always go away as fast as you want it to. Even though my plan was to come home and freelance so I could spend more time with my son before he started kindergarten, there was a white noise constantly in my head of those voices telling me I wasn't good enough.

As a result of that scar and listening to that noise, I spent most of that first year home working even harder than I did when I worked for someone else, proving to myself and those critics that I was good, that I could succeed. And I met my goal—that first year home I actually brought more income in as a freelancer than I had as a salaried employee in my old job.

But I didn't come close to spending the time I'd wanted with my son. At four years old, he literally played under my desk while I worked. I look back now at that time with regret because even though I went home that year, I wasn't really home. I'd let a scar steal my focus.

Where's Our Focus

This year Caleb turned thirteen. It's a little bewildering to think we finally have an official teenager in our midst since he's been pushing that direction for the last couple of years. This past year has been one of big changes and transition, watching my sweet little boy juggle hormones coming and going. One second he's wanting to cuddle up to watch a movie with me, and in the very next moment, he's storming off to watch TV by himself, annoyed by something I've done or breathed—it's hard to say sometimes. Moms of teenagers will understand.

He's now taller than I am, a fact he loves to frequently point out, but he also still loves to hug me, wrapping his arms around my shoulders (another subtle hint to his height change) and giving me a squeeze, and he still occasionally wants to hold my hand when we go for a walk. I can't complain much and will take every hug I can get.

I try not to live with a lot of regret or looking back wishing I'd done things differently, only because I believe God uses both our good and our bad experiences, our good and our bad choices, to get us where he needs us to be. When we stay focused on our scars, we can focus on regret, or a distraction from what we need to do to move on from them. Sometimes those scars can get in the way of what God wants us to do. Instead of letting go, we hold on, and we stop moving on.

> When we stay focused on our scars, we can focus on regret.

A long time passed before I could honestly say I'd moved on from the scar I received from my coworkers. We're talking years. Every project I attempted or every article I wrote, every book proposal I submitted and even after something got approved, even after I received an award or a check or a happy note from an editor, the doubt still lingered. The insecurity hung around. I stared at that scar in my mind's eye, rubbing it, unable to forget about it or let it go. And every time I hesitated in saying yes to something, or panicked or stressed on whether something I'd done was really good enough, the scar won. Even when I had success, I was hesitant to celebrate, remembering the reactions of my former colleagues when I showed excitement.

> God doesn't fail us! People fail us. Situations fail us. But God doesn't fail us.

Here's what I've learned over the last few years. Scars lose their power over us when we pay attention to the One who has all the power. I hope that doesn't sound like too much of a Sunday school answer, but it's true. God doesn't fail us! People fail us. Situations fail us. Choices by ourselves and by others can fail us. But God doesn't fail us, because his decisions aren't mistakes and his actions aren't by accident.

When I finally took my eyes off that scar and started putting my eyes on Jesus, on who he is and what he has done and does for me, I stopped worrying so much about the approval of others, and I started being a lot more concerned about his approval of me. I started realizing that Jesus asks for my availability, not my perfection. I can run to him like the psalmist says (Psalm 22:24) because he does not despise or detest us when we struggle or when we go through seasons of affliction. He listens when we cry to him for help. He gives us what we need to keep going.

What Story Will You Tell?

Caleb came home the other day from a birthday party where they'd played laser tag, and he proudly showed me a six-inch, bright red cut starting from the top of his left hand to just beyond the edge of his wrist. He'd scratched it on one of the gates going into the laser tag area, but he was already thinking of his answer when his friends at school asked him how he got it: "Hunting. I was hunting."

When I looked at him with an eyebrow (or both) raised, he shrugged, and with a big silly grin on his face, he said, "Come on,

Mom, chicks dig scars!" Oh brother. He's listened to his father too much.

Think about it, though. What's the most common reaction people have when they see a scar? "How did you get *that?*" In terms of nosiest questions, it ranks up there with "When are you due?" "What are you having?" and "Aren't you through having kids yet?" If the scar is serious enough—a bad burn or a disfiguring wound—they might not be so rude to ask. But they may still stare.

But how do we handle stories of our scars with other people? What about in church? It seems to me that all of us are so busy wanting and trying to convince other people to notice our scars, or our struggles, or our causes, things near and dear to us, that none of us are really listening to anyone else. We wring our hands and keep saying to ourselves, *If only other people would take time to hear me, if only other people would do more to help me…*

My husband has served in the Navy Reserves for over seventeen years and when we went through our first deployment, I spent most of that year thoroughly frustrated at the lack of care other people seemed to have for what our family was going through. Our small group at church (which wasn't very small—there were about fifty couples in it), a group we considered close family since we'd been with them for several years, acted as if Cliff had left for a two-week business trip instead of a ten-month tour to a combat zone. No one really asked about him and no one asked about us. I spent more time during that deployment noticing what wasn't done than being grateful for the things we did receive, whether it was a kind word or an occasional invitation for dinner. Though I knew we lived in an area with very few military families, I just didn't understand why other people weren't willing to help more, or at least speak up.

I realized, *I have no idea what to say.*

God gave me my first lesson in that, though, a couple of years later when our pastor's wife was diagnosed with cancer. She had a long journey ahead of her, filled with chemotherapy sessions and doctor appointments and other things I had no idea about. And I remember a specific moment one Sunday morning after church when I saw her down in the front of the sanctuary, looking a little worn down, and I made my way to her to give her a hug, and I realized, *I have no idea what to say.*

I'd never had cancer. I'd never had a close family member have cancer, and I had no idea what I could say that might encourage her, or if I just might have the opposite effect and say something stupid or thoughtless. That's when it finally clicked for me. Just as I struggled not knowing what to say to my friend with cancer, my friends who had never gone through deployment had no idea what to say to me either.

A few couples in our current church have gone through the hard and difficult task of international adoption over the last few years. It is a labor of love and a special calling God puts on a family to adopt a child, especially, perhaps, a child from another country. Dealing with red tape, disappointing delays, excruciating waits. One couple we know waited over three years from the time they got their referral to the time they got to bring home their little girl.

> We forget about God and we buy into the lie that we're completely alone.

I've noticed something in these families. They are passionate about their calling and their mission to be families to orphans, and they share that passion of international adoption with everyone else, in hopes it will become their passion too. So they post pictures on Facebook with cute slogans supporting adopting families or links to blog posts about how you as a friend can support your adopting friends. What struck me was that their efforts and their ways of asking for someone, anyone, to notice them weren't any different from what we military spouses do. We're all asking for someone to notice us. We're all looking for anyone who will "get us." We all want people in our corner who will help us, who will join in our fight, our cause, our passion, our pursuit of what's important to us.

But is there anyone who can "get us" better than God?

I think we can make two mistakes when we're dealing with scars. We can look to everyone else to help us heal our hurts, and when they can't, or won't, we give up. We can also convince ourselves that no one can help or be there for us, and so we don't even try. Either way, we forget about God and we buy into the lie that we're completely alone.

But we are not alone, and God has not abandoned us with our scars. Scars are proof that healing is happening. Remember that scar I mentioned earlier, the one I got while ironing? I can't even find it anymore. If I look really, really closely, I think I can just make it out. I think. The scar is just not there, not the way it was for years after that burn happened. Healing happened and the scar went away. But time was required.

> We need time for our emotional scars to heal too.

We need time for our emotional scars to heal too. Healing is a process, and forgiveness aids in that process. When we can let go of the hurt that caused the scar in the first place, we are that much closer to healing and moving on.

Five Ways to Start the Healing Process

1. **Recognize God's truth over your own.** Scars have a way of adding doubt, fear, and just plain old lies into our hearts and minds, which can be like an emotional cancer to our spirits. This is not the time to shy away from knowing and reading God's Word. Like the spiritual armor Ephesians 6 talks about, we need to surround ourselves with God's words of truth. Choose scriptures that have deep meaning for you. Memorize them and say them out loud as a reminder that God is bigger than your scars. Jeremiah 29:11 is often quoted in times of despair and pain:

   > "For I know the plans I have for you"—this is the Lord's declaration—"plans for your welfare, not for disaster, to give you a future and a hope."

   But look at what the following verses say:

   > "You will call to Me and come and pray to Me, and I will listen to you. You will seek Me and find Me when you search for Me with all your heart."

   God has plans for you, but those plans involve you. When the scars feel too big or seem too noticeable, don't give up. God doesn't, and he won't leave you by yourself to deal with them. But you must ask him for his help and trust him.

2. **Recognize what's happened to you and what needs to happen going forward.** I heard an interesting account recently of a man who started his life in a Romanian orphanage but was adopted by an American family when he was seven or eight years old. While his new family was loving and caring, the lack of love and care he experienced during those early formative years made it extremely difficult for him to accept the love and care from his new family. For much of

his adolescence and well into adulthood, he and his family had ongoing problems. Once he realized what had happened to him as a young child, he was able to better understand why he struggled with accepting love and kindness, and he gradually found ways to change his mind-set or reaction.

We don't have any control over what someone else has already done to us, but we do have control over how we respond today and what we do to move forward. You may have some days where you feel like you have no choice but to live and relive those experiences or circumstances that caused your scars, but oh, my sweet friend, you do. Not a choice dependent on your own strength and mind, but as you depend on God's strength, he gives you what you need to choose to take one step forward, and then another. Are you struggling with thinking every single day about a specific scar? Choose something else to think about when those thoughts threaten to invade by focusing on a blessing in your life as a reminder that good still happens and you can overcome the bad.

3. **Understand that scars signify healing that's already started.** Second Corinthians 5:17 assures us that anyone who has a relationship with Christ is "a new creation; old things have passed away, and look, new things have come." When we dwell on our scars, we can't move on. But God has so much more in store for you. Look beyond the scars. When you want to look backward, stop and make a list of everything you have to look forward to—and don't limit God! He is bigger than you and I will ever be able to comprehend. Thank him for the healing he is doing in your life, and for your new joys and hopes he's providing as you walk each day with him.

4. **Learn something from your scar.** Your lesson may be what *not* to do to other people or you may learn that God's given

you strength you didn't know you had. I think when we've been hurt deeply, our first instinct sometimes can be to prove a point—that we're not broken or we're not as affected as others might think. We might even try to ignore what's happened and push it as far down as possible. Learning something from our scars, though, requires humbling ourselves, as 1 Peter 5:6-7 tells us: "Humble yourselves, therefore, under the mighty hand of God, so that He may exalt you at the proper time, casting all your care on Him, because He cares about you." I love this verse because it's a promise—God lifts us up at just the right time. He is mighty, and he cares deeply for us.

5. **Trust God.** Sounds simple, but those two words can come with a lot of fear and hesitation. If we could just do this simple but profound act, each and every day, there would be no need for all the self-help books we see on store shelves. When I struggle to trust God in the process of healing my scars, I need to remember what Isaiah 55:9 says:

> "For as heaven is higher than earth,
>   so My ways are higher than your ways,
>   and My thoughts than your thoughts."

Surrender your scars. Let God use them for his purpose and ultimately for his glory and our joy.

5

When You're the One Who's Wrong

As we've discussed to this point, a lot of our hurts are legitimate. When someone does us wrong, our feelings can take over, controlling our actions and our responses. But sometimes, *we're* the ones in the wrong, and we still want to be the ones holding the grudges.

So as we dive into examining our own wrongs, our mistakes and slights and hurts we may have done toward others, I offer you a friendly word of warning: don't start reading this with your heels already dug in and your ears tightly covered with your hands. If there's something the Lord needs to work on your heart about, I pray that by the end of this chapter, you will be open to hearing exactly what he needs to say to you.

Let's just be real about what goes on in our heads sometimes. Thinking about everything "they" need to change or fix is a lot easier than thinking about what we need to fix. If you're married, you already know this is a common way we deal with conflict as couples, isn't it? If he would just do what he was supposed to do, there wouldn't be any problems, right? He probably thinks the same thing about you.

But this Blame the Other Guy game doesn't apply just in marriages. We do this with everyone. Friends, family, extended family, people at church, other parents at our kids' schools…we can become quite comfortable with the idea that *it's them and not us.*

85

So let me break it to you as gently as I can.

Sometimes it is them.

Sometimes it is us.

One of the earliest memories I have of doing something wrong is when I was in first grade and sat next to Travis, a nice guy, skinny, with freckles and curly light-brown hair that slightly puffed out like a cotton ball. One morning in class, we were working on our "All about me" packets, and both Travis and I were working on our self-portraits.

I remember bending down very intently as I painstakingly drew my head and then my face and, of course, my hair, because every six-year-old girl loves drawing hair. I only looked up as my teacher, Mrs. Moore, a plump woman with glasses and a general scowl on her face, walked past my desk. She absently glanced down at what I was doing, but her eyes and her lips smiled wide when she looked over at the desk next to mine.

"Travis! What a wonderful self-portrait!" she exclaimed, stopping to pick up his paper as she admired his artwork. "You are quite an artist."

As she handed the page back to Travis and walked back to her desk, I leaned across the aisle so I could get a better look at his picture. Yeah, the kid had some drawing chops. He got his curly hair right and, OK, his nose was pretty good. I looked back at mine. My teacher didn't even notice the buttons on my dress I'd drawn in as little hearts. I looked back at Travis and tapped my pencil on the desk, feeling frustrated. Then I had an idea.

"Hey Travis, want to trade pictures so you can look at mine and I can look at yours?" I asked him, a big smile on my face.

"Sure," he said, handing his paper to me as I handed him mine.

I glanced down at his picture. "You know," I said, picking up my brown crayon, "I think you need a few more freckles."

I wish I could freeze this moment. I wish I could get into a time machine and go back and speak to that little girl, or maybe pull that paper away from her, or at least the brown crayon. Thirty years later, this moment still stays with me. I'm not proud. I still don't really understand why I did it.

Very coyly, I started putting brown dots on the picture of his face where his freckles would be, and as Travis glanced over, eyebrows starting to furrow, my arm went wild.

The little brat colored all over his picture. (Oh wait, that brat was me.)

"Sara!"

My teacher came over and took the paper from me. I don't remember much of what happened next except there was a guaranteed promise of a phone call to my mother. And two days later I came down with the chicken pox. In my six-year-old mind, I wasn't sure if it was because I ate chicken that day in the cafeteria, or if God was teaching me a lesson for what I did to Travis. But there is no doubt that the dots all over my face for the next two weeks did teach me irony.

> We're human and we get it wrong, almost as much as we get it right.

Like that messy ruined picture, our actions toward others leave the same ruined effect in our hearts if we aren't careful. Relationships are messy, right? We're human and we get it wrong, almost as much as we get it right. But when we refuse to own up to our part in certain situations and conflicts, we don't do ourselves or the other people involved any good.

There were many times growing up I came home from school upset with my friends. Someone said something mean, or someone called a third-grade coup and no one wanted to play with me at recess. After moving several times through childhood, I learned that being the new kid had its advantages, but there were also disadvantages. I didn't always quite fit. Sometimes I *was* the square peg in the round hole. Problems with friends came up a lot. Feeling like an outsider always stayed near the surface of my heart.

After a tough day, my mother would try to make me feel better, sitting down with me and wiping away a tear or two. She'd say, "Sara, those girls are just jealous. You haven't done anything to deserve what they're doing, so don't think about them anymore. You're better off without them as friends." While I know she meant well, not ever learning to deal with conflict in a positive but effective way, always believing it was "them" and not me, set me up for more difficult lessons when I became an adult.

Saying You're Sorry

Have you ever known people who never apologize? Ever? As in *never*? Not in a meaningful, "I feel bad that I hurt you" kind of way. They may occasionally say sorry as in "I'm sorry you took it that way" or "I'm sorry you're so sensitive," but the problem is never really theirs.

That strategy is a good one, at least temporarily. If you're never sorry, you're never really responsible. Think about it. What do the big PR firms usually advise their clients when a scandal erupts? Offer sympathy for the situation, but never actually apologize—an apology might make people think you're actually in the wrong and willing to accept the blame.

That might work for companies but not for people. When you are never willing to apologize, you can't open the door to your heart for a relationship to move forward. You stay in some mental, formal living room chatting about the weather or news of the day, but what you miss out on are the heart-to-heart conversations that foster growth and deeper understanding of others and of yourself.

I don't think this era of social media we now live in, this nonstop "connecting" all of us do simply with the tips of our fingers, has helped. There was a story recently in the news about a young boy with Asperger's who had not made friends very easily at his school, and when his mom asked him which friends he wanted to invite to his upcoming birthday party, he told her no one because he didn't have any friends who would want to come. His mom was heart-broken he felt that way, as any mom would be, and so she created a Facebook page for his birthday, hoping to gather a few "likes" to show her son that people do care.

His story spread, and more than 1.4 million likes later and thou-sands of posts left on the page wall by kind people wishing him a happy birthday, I think the mom succeeded in what she set out to do. But there was criticism almost right away from others who pointed out that someone liking a page really doesn't equal a friend. There's some truth there. While I don't think it was the mom's inten-tion to tell her son he has 1.4 million friends—more to show him that there are people who care—how many others do get caught up in the friends number game with Facebook, Twitter, and every other social media flavor of the day? The higher your number, the more friends you have, right?

I found this to be true with my own experience on Facebook. While I first loved getting friend requests from women who had read my books, and slowly watched my friend number climb into the thousands, I noticed it got harder and harder to see my true friends in my news feed and know what they were up to. What was worse, when I shared things about my family, sometimes really inconse-quential things like what we were having for dinner, or sometimes frustrating things like not getting a response from a teacher, all of these comments would come in, offering opinions or criticisms. I realized very few of those people actually knew me, and I didn't know them. There was no real personal connection there to draw from. So I made some changes. My readers could connect with me on a public page, but my profile needed to be reserved for friends and family I actually knew—those people I worked with, I did life with, who I sometimes saw in person for lunch or at church.

I understand the argument that you can still develop great friendships online. I will always be grateful for the online forum of military wives I belonged to during our first deployment when Cliff was in Iraq. Since I knew no other military wives where we lived, at least at the beginning, those ladies who I knew only by usernames were a lifeline, a group I could turn to and ask questions and vent when I got frustrated and hadn't heard from my husband in weeks and cry with when it all felt too much. But here was the reality check for me: I only knew those women from what they were willing to share, and they only knew the same about me.

The dirty little secret not all of us are comfortable admitting about why we like online friendships so much is that they are a whole lot easier to disconnect from if things don't work out. Don't like what your friend says about a sports team you've cheered for since you were two years old? Hate it when your more liberal friend, or your more conservative friend, posts in-your-face, one-sided political messages, especially around election time, and they're clearly voting for a candidate you are not? What about the friend who shares "rescue this dog before he ends up in dog heaven" pictures so often her profile makes you hear Sarah McLachlin's song that starts, "In the arms of the angel…" from that commercial of poor abused puppies and kitties every single time you look at her page? Or how about the friend who cannot quit with the pitches for her new direct sales business she's SO EXCITED about? (And sends you fifty invitations to her next fifty shows, which are all on the other side of the country.)

> We don't value relationships in the same way we used to.

You get aggravated. You get annoyed, and you start thinking…maybe you just weren't meant to be friends. So you hide those friends from your news feed. Or you just cut the cord completely and hit that "defriend" or "unfollow" button. They didn't really mean that much to you anyway.

That's where I think social media has hurt us the most. We don't value relationships in the same way we used to. We've convinced ourselves that our opinion really does matter a lot more than the opinions of others, and we have the "likes" to prove it. Or we've bought into maybe the worst lie of all—"I can say whatever I want because *it's my page.*"

I'm guilty of this. Big time. And it has cost me friendships. *Real* friendships.

Our son hasn't had the easiest time in seventh grade. As I write this, we are in the second semester of it, and Cliff has been away on his third deployment in Afghanistan and Bahrain respectively, for Caleb's entire school year.

Caleb's never been a straight *A* student, but middle school has rocked his world for the worse. Like a lot of boys, the organizational skills haven't fully developed yet, and his grades have been average to not so good. Though we've never had discipline problems with him in school, we have had attention and focus issues to deal with. At a time in a boy's life when he starts to really want his dad around a whole lot more than his mom, when hormones have kicked in and he is now taller than his mom (and sometimes just as moody), Caleb hasn't had the blessing of having Cliff around to help sort out the complicated, ever-changing thoughts that are the life of an almost-teenager.

Compared to the last two deployments, on an "I'm freaking out, I'm stressing out" meter with one being the lowest and ten the highest, for the most part I've stayed around a four or lower. God has been there, every day and every month my husband has been away, and I've sensed his peace and his love surrounding our lives and my heart. I've been able to just keep taking one day at a time, serving him as we wait for our family to be reunited.

Most days I can say that.

There have been a few I cannot.

Take for example the first few weeks of the school year. By the end of sixth grade, we knew Caleb needed some motivation to get his homework written down each and every day, so we set a requirement in place that he had to get his homework planner signed off by each teacher. We needed to know he was paying attention and he was participating in class. He needed the accountability. Each teacher initialed on the respective day in his planner if he was doing those things, and if he was not, they didn't. We knew (and Caleb knew) if a teacher's initial was missing, a family discussion would follow.

Since the system worked pretty well at the end of sixth grade, Cliff and I decided we shouldn't mess with progress, and at the beginning of Caleb's seventh grade year, we asked his new teachers to do the same thing. Our plan was that if all went well, after the end of the first nine weeks, Caleb wouldn't have to go to his teachers for initials. That was our plan anyway.

The teachers had another plan, and there was a little bit of a complication. One of Caleb's teachers was also a family friend, a benefit, I initially thought. But things took a different direction than I expected when she stopped by my house one day after school to talk about Caleb's homework planner. She told me she and the other teachers had talked, and they didn't think it was necessary for them to sign off on Caleb's planner each day. He seemed to be doing fine, and really, this was the year kids needed to learn more about personal responsibility, and he wasn't going to do that if he had to check in with the teachers every day.

> I wanted to disagree. I wanted to say no. But I didn't.

Cliff wasn't there for me to talk to about it (he was already with his unit mobilizing for his deployment), and I took what our friend was saying to mean that maybe I was doing a little too much parent quarterbacking at this point in Caleb's studies. I wanted to disagree. I wanted to say no. But I didn't. I was afraid to be thought of as a less-than-perfect parent.

Against my better judgment, I told her OK. Caleb didn't have to get initials each day. Within the first week or two, Caleb stopped writing anything down at all.

After a few weeks of watching the good grades he'd started the year with quickly tank into *D*s and *F*s, despite my best efforts to keep the accountability going at home, I let my frustration turn into fear, fear that under my watch he was going to flunk out of seventh grade and his dad was going to come home with hands up in the air, asking me, "What happened?"

Then my fear turned into anger that I was even put into this position to begin with. What would have been the harm in just letting him do what we'd asked? After checking his grades online one day and seeing yet another message that said, "Your child has a FAILING GRADE today," lit up big and bold as soon as I logged on, I'd had enough. I'd hit my breaking point. My anger quickly turned into a mama bear's wrath.

What I'd feared would happen, happened. I should have stood up for my boy. But because our friend was on Caleb's teaching team, I was afraid to say that this wasn't working and we needed to go back to what we'd done before.

Instead, I did what a lot of us do these days when we're upset and feel like we have no way for anyone to hear us. I got on Facebook and got ready to type the most passive-aggressive status I could think of.

(Here is where I think Facebook could really help a lot of us out. They seem so intent on knowing everything about us anyway…why couldn't they also include a little question that pops up when we're about to hit that little post button that says, I don't know, something like, *Are you sure you want to post this? Is it really your intention to say exactly what you think and risk hurting feelings of people you care about?* Or they could keep it even shorter and sweeter, maybe with a Southern twang thrown in for good measure: *Are you sure about that, honey?* Unfortunately, Facebook hasn't come up with a permission-granted, second-chances button just yet.)

Telling Facebook or Twitter isn't any better than telling another friend what you hate about someone or something, or how you don't understand the friend, or the situation, especially if you're not willing to tell that person to their face.

Though I never mentioned names or specifics, I used a social media site to let out all my frustration over this situation. (Sounds as silly as it is, doesn't it?) I explained how I felt like a team of teachers had overlooked our wishes as parents for our student, and my friends responded (as I'd hoped they would—why else do we post half the things we do?) with sympathy and empathy.

Then my teacher friend also commented. Suddenly, the outpouring of my soul on Facebook didn't feel so good. She was offended. I was surprised she'd decided to comment publicly since I hadn't used her name or said anything about her directly. But her decision to comment just made me all the more indignant, and so I fired back (in such a grown-up, big girl manner) that I was venting over a situation I found frustrating because *this was my page to do with as I pleased.* (If I'd thought of it, I'd probably have thrown in a "So there!" just for the added effect. Can't you see the virtual foot stomping?)

Do you know what it means when we vent? We think of it as a way to get out strong emotions instead of bottling them up. But appliance companies have a different definition: it's a way to get rid of a whole bunch of hot air.

> Venting doesn't do us any good. Talking does.

Certain friends I've had over the years can remember meeting me, and some of my first words to them were "Do you mind if I just vent for a second?" They thought it was quirky and honest and cute; when I think about it now, I just see it as selfish.

Oh my gracious stars. Jesus, what you must think when we act the way we want to and not in a way that's pleasing to you. When we say things without thinking and do things that don't reflect you or what you care about.

I've become convinced, only because I've seen more hurt than help happen, that venting doesn't do us any good. Talking does. Sitting down with someone does. You think before you talk. You don't think before you vent.

Remember that scene between Joe (Tom Hanks) and Kathleen (Meg Ryan) in *You've Got Mail*? The one where over instant messaging, Kathleen mourns that she isn't good at saying exactly what she wants to, at the exact moment she'd like? Joe proposes that if he could pass all of his mean comments to her, he would never be ugly to someone, she could be as ugly as she wanted, and they'd "both be happy." But Joe also gives her a warning: "On the other hand…when you finally have the pleasure of saying the thing you mean to say at the moment you mean to say it, remorse inevitably follows."

There's a whole lot of truth in that.

I was angry. But after I finally started cooling down a little, I was also regretful. I knew I'd made a bad choice, and I knew I needed to fix things with my friend. I got back on Facebook and wrote a long private message to her. I hoped my honesty with her would open a new line of communication between us. I realize now that I should have asked to speak to her face-to-face. In response, I got an email letting me know that I'd hurt her with what I'd said on Facebook. She also let me know that for professional reasons she'd defriended me.

> You can choose to do the right thing, even if it's following a wrong choice—especially if it follows a wrong choice.

I understood, and I regretted that my behavior had led to it.

Apologizing for something we've done wrong is never without risk—there's always the chance the person we're apologizing to isn't going to respond the way we want. But looking at it from their perspective, the actions we took or the words we spoke, the reason our apology was needed in the first place, might not have been what they wanted either.

So you can't control whether someone forgives you, or the extent they are willing to forgive you. But you can control what you do. You can choose to do the right thing, even if it's following a wrong choice—especially if it follows a wrong choice.

Jesus tells a story in Matthew 18 about a slave who owed an enormous debt to a king and could not pay it back. The king insisted the slave sell himself, his wife, his kids, everything he had, to pay back the debt, but the slave begged for the king's mercy. The king had compassion on the slave and forgave his debt. That same slave, though, later found someone who owed him a much smaller debt and demanded his payment, showing no mercy to the friend but throwing him into prison until he could pay every penny back. The slave had learned nothing from the grace previously shown to him, and when the king found out, he took the slave and tortured him until he could pay back every penny that he owed.

Aren't we tempted sometimes to be like that slave? We beg God to pour out his grace on us, but we're resistant sometimes to give grace to others. In my situation with my friend, as much as I wish that things were different, that we were closer, I cannot hold a grudge now toward her if we're not. I can't say, "Well, I apologized so now she's the one with the problem." She's not and it doesn't work that way. I fully recognize what I did to cause a rift in our friendship. Grace must be given because God gives grace to me.

> When we're not willing to ask forgiveness from others, we will be less willing to offer forgiveness.

I continue to hope that one day our friendship will be better, and as time has passed, I've seen our communication slowly improve. Our families are spending time together again. Maybe that's another important factor to consider: allowing time for heated emotions to settle and hard feelings to lessen.

Jesus made his expectations of forgiveness for us very clear when he told his disciples that when they prayed, they needed to be sure to forgive anyone they had a problem with "so that your Father in heaven will also forgive you your wrongdoing. But if you don't forgive, neither will your Father in heaven forgive your wrongdoing" (Mark 11:25-26).

When we're not willing to ask forgiveness from others, we will be less willing to offer forgiveness. When we aren't willing to forgive others, we have a harder time understanding God's forgiveness and his grace toward us. That understanding helps us realize the importance of depending on him instead of depending on ourselves.

Do You Hear Him?

We've all had moments where we've said something we wish we hadn't, when we've intentionally or unintentionally hurt someone and then immediately regretted it. But so much of where we find ourselves in the wrong could have been avoided in the first place if we'd willingly listened before we acted. When I think about my actions that day, blowing up on Facebook, telling the world instead of talking to a friend, I know that a lot of it could have been prevented if I'd done just one little thing first.

> What if I had prayed?

What if I had prayed?

What if, when faced with letting my thoughts loose, I'd taken a moment to first turn those thoughts and those feelings over to God? Would I have been so quick to hit that post button then? Or would I have more likely pressed that delete key instead?

Isn't that what might have happened if I'd just listened?

The truth is I was upset. I was hurt. I was frustrated and concerned and feeling a little wobbly from it all. But instead of getting on my knees and asking God for wisdom, I just hit the keys—and set in motion a chain reaction I couldn't take back.

But when we have a relationship with Jesus, we are not left on our own in these kinds of circumstances. When you feel like you've been wronged, or you've wronged someone else, you aren't alone to figure out what to do. When you know Jesus, you have his Spirit in you. Paul asked the Corinthian church, "Don't you yourselves know that you are God's sanctuary and that the Spirit of God lives in you?" (1 Corinthians 3:16). The psalmist asked God to use his Spirit to teach him God's will and to lead him on "level ground" (Psalm 143:10). This means we have a source for wisdom when we need it, but we have to be willing to listen for that voice in order to hear it and to heed it.

So how do we hear from the Holy Spirit?

We're not talking about listening for an audible voice (because if you're hearing voices inside your head—with names and accents and attitudes—well, there's an entirely different book you should be reading right now). But we are talking about a spiritual conviction that comes over us when we ask God to help us know what we're to do. I know there was something inside me that day that said, "Wait. Stop. This isn't the way to handle this." By ignoring God's Spirit, and just going ahead and doing what I wanted, I was saying I knew better, I wanted things my way. I was angry, and I wanted other people to know it.

But this isn't God's way. This isn't his plan. This isn't what he asks us to do when he calls us to forgive, and over and over, he tells us in his Word, we are to forgive. Even when we feel wronged. When we feel like it's the other person's fault. And when we're wrong? We need to ask for forgiveness as well.

Asking for forgiveness isn't easy. As I've mentioned before, there's a risk that forgiveness won't really be given. Several years ago I found myself jealous of another author, an acquaintance I'd gotten to know online. We'd talked by phone a few times, connected through email and Facebook, and had what I considered a good professional working relationship. But as I saw her become more and more successful, achieving certain goals and receiving opportunities I'd wished for myself, I found myself more and more envious, to the point where I avoided her and refused her offers of connection. Instead of seeing her as a friend, I saw her as competition. I was as green toward her as the walls in my office I'm now writing in.

> I knew it was wrong. I knew that the Holy Spirit grieved every time I had a jealous thought or a mean response in my head.

I knew it was wrong. I knew that the Holy Spirit grieved every time I had a jealous thought or a mean response in my head, even if I never said it out loud. But I ignored it.

So God got my attention in a very specific way.

My first book to write as a solo author, not as a collaborator or a ghost writer, was published, and I was so excited. The book had been out for only about a week when one of the local news stations covered the story. This was the same news station that had covered our family the year before when we'd gone through Cliff's first deployment. They'd shared a series of stories about us, living the ups and downs of a military family whose service member was away. During that time, another military wife on the other side of the city contacted me through my husband's civilian job, wanting to encourage me with a book she'd self-published about deployment. I'd thanked her for the gift and for her thoughtfulness, but never really read it or gave it much thought, mainly due to a busy schedule.

After watching the news report that my book had released, my husband gave me a celebratory hug and told me how proud he was of me.

"Pull it up on Amazon," he said. "I want to see it."

As I did, I noticed there was already a review for it.

"Wow, that's weird," I said.

And then my heart sank. It was a one-star review, the lowest of the low. I recognized the name of the military wife who had sent me her book—the book I'd never really looked at. The blood drained from my face as I clicked on the link and read her review, which implied that the ideas in my book were not my own. The words cut into my heart no less painfully than if she had used a knife. I'd pored over my book as I'd written it. I had deliberated over and prayed about every word and every sentence, and all I'd wanted to do was encourage military wives to lean on God's strength.

> My celebration felt short-lived, like someone had come into our house and dumped my imaginary celebratory cake on the floor and stomped on it.

The tears started. My celebration felt short-lived, like someone had come into our house and dumped my imaginary celebratory cake on the floor and stomped on it. Although I knew this reviewer's implication was untrue, my heart was sick for another reason. I sensed her hurt from having poured out her own story, only to see someone else put out a similar story with perhaps better results.

And that's where God got me.

I might not have posted about it on a public website, but I'd had similar feelings toward my author friend. Jealousy. Envy at her success. Twinges of frustration at things that seemed unfair.

Even as I was still wiping away the tears, I knew that frustration and understood those feelings the reviewer had launched through cyberspace. I could see them in her because I knew they were in me. I couldn't do anything about this woman's feelings, but I knew there was something I could do about my own. I knew I needed to make my own heart right.

After I'd talked to my agent the next day, I felt a little better about the negative review. She'd looked at both books and saw no connection between the two except that they were both based around the same themes of faith and deployment. "You can't hold a copyright on an idea," she told me. There was nothing I could do about the review, and she did not recommend that I contact the woman as I first suggested.

As I hung up the phone, I got ready to make another phone call. I sat at my desk, looking at the number I needed to dial and praying about the words I wanted to say. This wasn't going to be an easy thing to do, but I needed to do it.

When the phone began ringing, I got nervous. *What if she thinks I'm crazy? What if she thinks worse of me once I tell her I was jealous of her? What if this is all a really bad idea?*

But I knew it wasn't a bad idea. I knew God had told me to make it right and that whether she responded favorably or not, this was less about my friend and more about my obedience to my heavenly Father and making it right with him. I thought about the words in Psalm 51:10 (ESV),

> Create in me a clean heart, O God,
> and renew a right spirit within me.

For his Spirit to work in me, my heart has to be free from the junk my human nature wants to collect and hold on to—selfish traits like jealousy and envy and spite, those characteristics that start and end with the question, "What about me?"

> For his Spirit to work in me, my heart has to be free from the junk my human nature wants to collect and hold on to.

My friend answered the phone, a little surprised to hear from me, but sweet and pleasant just the same. After a little small talk, I shakily dived into why I was calling and what I needed to tell her. I was sorry for my attitude, sorry for my negative feelings toward her, and I hoped she could forgive me.

She was surprised by my confession because she'd never noticed or felt any ill will from me, but she appreciated my honesty and apology and accepted it with graciousness and kindness. After we hung up, I said a short prayer of thanks to God for speaking to me and for helping me.

We're instructed in James 5:16 to confess our sins "to one another and pray for one another…The urgent request of a righteous person is very powerful in its effect." My desire is to be righteous in God's eyes and to follow after his righteousness. I'm going to fail in that effort because none of us can be righteous on our own. Only with God's help, and his grace, can we see his righteousness in our hearts and our lives.

> Only with God's help, and his grace, can we see his righteousness in our hearts and our lives.

We are going to make mistakes. We are going to find ourselves in the midst of wrongs. What we do after those mistakes is the question. Do we give up, believing that we'll never make it right? Or do we deal with what God asks for us to address, doing the right thing, asking for forgiveness when needed, and giving forgiveness even when it's undeserved?

Five Reasons to Ask for Forgiveness Right Now

1. **A heart of peace is easier to live with than a heart of spite or guilt.** Romans 14:19 reminds us to pursue what "promotes peace and what builds up one another." If you know someone is upset with you, whether you think they are justified in their feelings, make attempts to resolve the conflict. Go to that person and ask for their forgiveness. Be sincere in your efforts. If they do not respond or return your attempt to make peace, then you will at least know you did everything you could to make the relationship or situation better. Then be at peace with that.

2. **Choosing humility before pride is the better choice.** You'll always learn something when you deliberately put someone else's feelings before your own and you're willing to confess that you were wrong. But when you allow your pride to get in the way, maybe by refusing to see the other person's side of things, Proverbs 11:2 tells us disgrace is sure to follow. Jesus said that in his kingdom many who are first will be last and the last will be first. Those who are willing to ask for forgiveness recognize it's less about our feelings than it is about bringing honor to the Lord in everything we do.

3. **Pretending nothing's wrong will make you weary.** "When I kept silent, my bones became brittle from my groaning all day long" (Psalm 32:3). Holding on to wrongs that you have done to someone else, or even being aware of hard feelings that you know someone is holding toward you, can wear you down emotionally and add stress and tension to your life. If you know there's a problem, address it, and don't wait for the perfect time; just choose a good time. Trust that God will give you the words to say and the right attitude in which to say them.

4. **Holding on to sin in your life or hurt you're responsible for makes it harder to keep a close relationship with God.** It's difficult to come to God each morning with a thankful open heart when you've closed part of it off because of unresolved sin or conflict, whether with God himself or with someone else. Hebrews 10:22-23 says for us to "draw near [to God] with a true heart in full assurance of faith, our hearts sprinkled clean from an evil conscience and our bodies washed in pure water. Let us hold on to the confession of our hope without wavering, for He who promised is faithful."

5. **You may be the only Jesus people see.** Jesus tells us in Matthew 5 to let our lights shine before others so they can "see your good works and give glory to your Father in heaven." But when we've wronged someone and we don't ask for forgiveness as soon as we realize it, they don't see Jesus or one of his children. They just see someone pretending to be like Jesus when it's convenient and acting like everybody else when it's not.

6

Holding On to Hurts

There's a series on television right now about a young woman who has returned to her childhood home with only one thing on her mind: to avenge her father's wrong conviction and subsequent death at the hands of a group of evil, selfish people. Under a false identity, she integrates herself into their circle and their family, and through complicated plots and schemes, finds ways to successfully destroy careers, reputations, relationships, and lives.

But not everything goes according to her plans. She finds as she goes after the people she has so much hatred and resentment toward, the people in her life she does love and treasure sometimes get caught in the cross fire.

Cliff and I chatted one night by text message while I watched an episode, and he asked me what I thought about the series. "Forgiveness is a whole lot easier," I wrote. "And not nearly as many people die."

When we don't forgive, something dies. Something moves closer to the edge of death. A relationship, usually. A friendship. A family member you no longer see or talk to.

Something dies within us too. Hope. Trust. Mercy. Compassion. All qualities we need and can't afford to lose.

We have to stop holding on to our hurts. We have to figure out ways to let them go. That noise, that white noise we've talked about that drowns out God's voice and encourages us to wallow in our hurts instead of forgiving and moving on, we need to figure out ways to ignore it.

We need to turn the white noise off.

So how do we do that?

We start by addressing the question that is always present when we're talking about hurts. The question that rests on our hearts, whispered in our minds, sometimes written in jagged, crooked letters in journals and diaries, and sometimes when we just don't feel like anyone hears us anymore, we scream it from our lips or softly say in tearful prayers, *What about me?*

What about me?

Don't I count?

Don't you care?

Does everyone else always have to be first? Don't I get a chance to be line leader today? Can't I be the one who's special and important and acknowledged for a change? Does God even see me? Does he even hear me? Why are my hurts any less significant than someone else's?

So really, tell me, what about me?

> Our question needs to change from "What about me?" to "What about him?"

Most of the time, when we ask this question, we're never going to get the answer we're looking for. We're never going to find full satisfaction, maximum contentment, or absolute fulfillment because our full satisfaction can never be reached when our goal ends with us. Our full satisfaction can come only when we start acknowledging that our fulfillment, our contentment, comes only when we're pursuing God's will for our lives. Our question needs to change from "What about me?" to "What about him?"

This isn't easy, and it doesn't even *sound* good, right? I mean, if you're looking for Sunday school answers, sure. Asking "What about God?" is the right question to ask. We're supposed to put Jesus first.

We're supposed to follow God with all our heart, mind, and spirit. We're supposed to floss before we go to bed every night, too, but that doesn't always happen either. We know the benefits—but sometimes we're unwilling to do what we're supposed to do because, well, we don't want to.

The human will is one hard cookie. We can hold on to things for years with no resolution or progress, just the thought. An idea, plans, dreams—we can hold tight to all of it if we get it into our heads and our hearts. The hold we have on our hurts can also be hard to break.

My husband told me a story the other day, one you may have heard before, about the way hunters catch wild monkeys in Africa. They'll take a coconut or a cantaloupe, hollow it out with a hole just slightly bigger than the monkey's hand, put a banana or maybe some peanuts inside, and hang it from a tree. When the monkey comes along, he sticks his hand inside the narrow hole to grab the treat he's discovered, but he gets a surprise when he realizes by making a fist around his prize, he can no longer pull his hand out of the hole. He's stuck. He's trapped.

To escape before the hunters come to collect him, he just needs to let go of the food; once he does, he can pull his hand out and go on about his business. But he won't. He gives up his freedom, and most likely his life, because he refuses to walk away from what he's holding on to.

That's a perfect illustration of what happens when we hold on to our hurts and refuse to let them go. Our hurts do not trap us. We trap ourselves with our hurts. We close ourselves in, convinced that nothing can be different, that nothing in our lives will change, and we're left asking *what about me?* over and over as we hold on to our hurts and look around at everyone else who doesn't seem to be caught or stuck or tied down like we are.

Even as I write about letting go of our hurts, this is something I

> Our hurts do not trap us. We trap ourselves with our hurts.

personally struggle with. There are hurts in my life I want to hold on to. I get weighed down by other people's unfairness and selfishness and thoughtlessness, and those thoughts can sometimes all pile up at once in my heart, running through my mind like a YouTube clip, reminding me over and over of all the ways I've been slighted or ignored or mistreated. And that little voice keeps saying *what about me?*

When you encourage others in their hard times, but you don't see anyone reaching out to you in your times of need…

When you ask for help and no one responds…

When you share something on your heart and it's just ignored…

Sometimes you just want to give up. You want to hold on to those hurts, hide behind your door, and not try anymore. Just now I had to pray and confess some hurts that threatened to overwhelm my heart today, and Jesus brought the words to my mind from Galatians 6:9—"So we must not get tired of doing good, for we will reap at the proper time if we don't give up."

There's also a second part to that Scripture—life is not just about us. Verse 10 says: "Therefore, as we have opportunity, we must work for the *good of all*, especially for those who belong to the household of faith" (emphasis mine).

> God cares very much. He will put people in our paths to remind us of that fact.

When we refuse to let hurts go, we miss out on opportunities to serve God, to let him work through us and to see him work in us. We can miss blessings and overlook his gifts. We can become convinced no one cares. But God cares very much. He will put people in our paths to remind us of that fact. He will also put people in our paths to challenge us.

Proverbs 19:11 states that "a person's insight gives him patience, and his virtue is to overlook an offense." Virtue in this case means literally "a beautiful adornment." When we have enough understanding of God's bigger picture in our lives and the lives of others, we can have more patience and, in turn, more willingness to disregard what someone does or doesn't do, says or doesn't say. That willingness, in God's eyes, is a beautiful display of his love in us. I like how the GOD'S WORD translation puts it:

> A person with good sense is patient,
>   and it is to his credit that he overlooks an offense.

Don't we all need more good sense?

So how do we learn to overlook our hurts? Do we just become robots, vowing never to feel? Or is there something deeper we need to grasp? Is it just a matter of gaining more sense?

Let's pause here and unpack this Scripture a little more, because I believe there are some great truths in this one simple proverb we can apply when we want to let go of our hurts.

Insight

We find some cause-and-effect things happening with this verse. Insight develops patience. Patience gives us an ability to overlook what normally might offend us. But it all goes back to insight.

To have insight is to discern or perceive the true nature of something. The truth we must recognize and remember when we're tempted to hold on to hurts is that our value and worth come from God—not from those who slight us or criticize us or ignore us or treat us in ways we wish they wouldn't.

> Our value and worth come from God—not from those who slight us or criticize us.

God made you "remarkably and wonderfully" (Psalm 139:14), with plans for you, to give you a "future and a hope" (Jeremiah 29:11), and saved you, not because of what you could do, but because of what Christ did for you, "so that having been justified by His grace, we may become heirs with the hope of eternal life" (Titus 3:7). You are made in his image (Genesis 1:27), and he "rewards those who seek Him" (Hebrews 11:6) and "who put their hope in His faithful love" (Psalm 147:11). That's how valuable you are to God.

So when we understand our worth to God, we don't have to rely on the approval or disapproval of others, we don't have to worry about what other people do for us or don't do for us. We're loved, period, and the love God gives us is a love that can't be equaled by anyone else. But to fully understand his love, we need to understand his Word, and that means keeping his Word in front of us constantly and consistently so we can learn and apply his teachings, live out his truths, and live for him alone.

In 2 Timothy 3:16-17 we're reminded, "All Scripture is inspired by God and is profitable for teaching, for rebuking, for correcting, for training in righteousness, so that the man of God may be complete, equipped for every good work." When we study his Word, we can be prepared and ready to deal with the hurts that come. Just having insight won't prevent us from getting hurt. There isn't some metal armor we can pull on to keep darts and arrows from piercing us every now and then. But when we know God's truth, we can apply it and let go of those hurts more quickly.

Patience

> We don't have to take everything so personally.

When God gives us insight, he helps us hold people's reactions or actions toward us at arm's length. We don't have to take everything so personally. The patience that comes with insight gives us a new perspective with the expectations we put on others. I stop expecting people to behave perfectly—or at least the way I think they should. I stop expecting them to act toward me in a certain way. When I practice patience, I practice an understanding that people aren't perfect, and they are flawed human beings. Just like me.

This is hard, especially if the same hurt comes up over and over from the same people, and there's no resolution, there's no willingness to meet halfway, maybe there's not even a willingness to sit down and have a conversation.

You may have someone in your family who knows exactly how to push your hurt button. Maybe they don't see things the same way you see them, and so they see you as different and not worth the time to understand. Instead of trying to understand you, they just ignore you and make you feel like you're invisible rather than a part of things. They don't ask about your day or your job or anything that's important to you. Or they gloss over things that you see as important, and they make you feel insignificant and not worth their time. The more the cycle spins, the more hurt you get, and the more angry or bitter or frustrated you become. You hold on to the hurt.

> When we lower our expectations of people and increase our trust in God, we worry less about what people do and more about what God wants us to do.

Stop holding things that aren't yours to hold on to. Realize that whatever those people in your life are doing, however they're behaving, doesn't have anything to do with you. There's something in their hearts, their lives that they're not dealing with. This is where patience comes in. When we lower our expectations of people and increase our trust in God, we worry less about what people do and more about what God wants us to do and how he wants us to respond in every situation.

So practice patience. The next time a person in your life does something to you that's a recurring hurt, pause and *change your perspective*. You know what I'm talking about—this could be your mother who's always asking you why you're still single, or your father who can't understand why you don't have a "real job" yet, or a family member or friend who comments about your wardrobe choices, or a coworker who always leaves you out of the group invite for lunch. Look at that person, not through your eyes, but through God's. What do you see? Someone who's missing something? Someone who may not even know him? Someone whose own hurts are preventing them from fully living in God's peace?

When you ask those questions with that person in mind, you should feel a little change in your emotions, a little softening, a little of the hurt slightly lifting away. Our eyes see one way, but God's eyes see something different. The more we embrace patience toward others, looking at them the way God looks at them, the more we can let go of some of these hurts we find holed up in our hearts.

Overlook the Offense

We have to stop taking things so personally. When we develop the patience for other people, we can also develop the skill to overlook what they do to offend us. Being offended by others is not a new problem. The author of Ecclesiastes says it pretty plainly: "Don't pay attention to everything people say, or you may hear your servant cursing you, for you know that many times you yourself have cursed others" (Ecclesiastes 7:21-22). I think his point is worth applying here. Other people are going to say hurtful things, and we should know, because we've said them ourselves.

Why can't I just move on, start fresh, and be renewed in him?

So how do we overlook the hurts? This isn't the same as going to the store and avoiding the candy aisle. Saying we can overlook when someone does something to upset us, and actually succeeding, well, it's a lot easier to say than do, isn't it?

I mentioned earlier that I've struggled with some of my own hurts this week as I've worked on this chapter. It's always so like God to put my feet to the fire with what I'm writing and what he's teaching me. Earlier today, I was struggling so much with my self-perceived hurts that I had to take a break and go for a walk in the sunshine. As I walked around my neighborhood, thinking about the nagging frustration that keeps darkening my spirit (and in turn coming out in my attitude with my family and others), I asked God to help me understand why I just can't seem to let this particular hurt go. Why can't I just move on, start fresh, and be renewed in him?

He put three thoughts in my heart that I believe you can benefit from as well. If you are struggling to let hurts go, or to overlook a specific offense from someone else, I hope these practical steps will help.

1. Stop putting words of value to your hurt.

Every time you talk about what's bothering you or who is hurting you, what they're doing to you, you give that hurt power over your heart and your life, and you crank up the white noise to full volume. You give the enemy more room to do more damage.

When you talk about it with your best friend over the phone or sob over it with your husband or tell your entire Bible study group over and over the wrong that's been done to you, you aren't moving on. You aren't letting it go.

Let me make this clear, though. I'm not saying you should never talk about your hurt; what I am saying is when we continually talk about our hurt without looking for resolution and closure, when we dwell on the hurt and the pain it's caused, and we don't give that hurt to the Lord and leave it with him, we don't move on. We don't let go. It becomes impossible to overlook the offense that's been done to us.

> Pray for the person who's responsible for the hurt.

So talk with your spouse or a trusted friend or family member about your hurt, and then resolve to leave it with God. Pray over it, asking him to remove it from your life and trust that he already has. Pray for the person who's responsible for the hurt. God will use your prayer to not only make a difference in that person's life but in your heart as well.

2. Stop giving more credit to the hurt than it deserves.

We can let hurts take over our lives, and there is no reason for it. People do this sometimes in a job when they lose an account or they fail to close a deal or they're short in sales numbers or income for the month. Maybe someone says something, someone close to them, and they're hurt and believe that what's been said is true. Instead of taking a breath, acknowledging the mistake, and moving on, they wallow in the mistake, they stagger around with the hurt, and it just follows them. They can't seem to recover.

We already know God is bigger than any hurt, and he controls our future. So stop letting the hurt control your life, and instead, give your life back to God. Ask him to remove the hurt and help you find ways to move forward. Focus on what he wants you to know, what he wants to show you.

3. Stop allowing room in your heart for the hurt.

Fill that space with the knowledge and the love of Christ instead. If you have tried everything you can to resolve an issue between you and someone else, and they've refused your attempts, they won't apologize or acknowledge the hurt, do what Matthew 18:17 says— "let him be like an unbeliever and a tax collector to you." Do you really think much about the tax man? Maybe once a year? Apply the same principle here to the person who hurt you.

Holding on to hurts never hurts the person responsible for hurting us; we're the ones who are affected. Even as I write that, though, I realize that sometimes other people *are* impacted. Our families, our children, or others who love us and want the best for us—those relationships can be influenced when we hold on to a hurt. Because we cling to the pain we once felt, we let that pain impact everything else. How many families have been affected because a hurt that occurred generations ago has been passed down from grandmother to mother to daughter to granddaughter? What difference would that family have experienced if the hurt had just been let go in the generation where it happened?

When we can't let go of our hurts, we miss one very important fact: this life isn't about us. My life is not my own when I commit it to Christ.

Your life belongs to God, and he already holds it firmly in his hands.

If you are a Christian, if you desire to follow Christ in your everyday, run-of-the-mill, eat-your-cornflakes-for-breakfast-and-fluff-your-pillow-before-you-head-to-bed life, the life you live today and every day is not your life to hold on to. Your life belongs to God, and he already holds it firmly in his hands. So that means your successes belong to God. That also means your hurts belong to him as well. As Paul so eloquently states in 1 Corinthians 7:23, we've been "bought at a price; do not become slaves of men." That's exactly what we do, though, when we don't let go of our hurts. We hand over the freedom we know through Christ to someone else who doesn't deserve it.

Sometimes I think we hold on to hurts because we're walking around in this emotional fog just trying to find someone who will understand our hurt. All we want is someone to acknowledge it, to make it right, to tell us it's OK and that things will get better. I think that's why we talk about our hurts so much, and we throw them out there in our conversations with friends or family or the cashier at the grocery store or anyone who will listen because *we just want someone to understand.*

He was loved, but he was also despised.

Dear sweet friend, you already have someone who understands.

Jesus understands, and those are not empty words. Jesus experienced hurts. He doesn't tell us to overlook or move on or let go of anything he hasn't already had to face in his own experience as fully God and fully man.

Think about it. He was loved, but he was also despised. There were crowds who loved him and wanted to hang on every word he said, and there were crowds who wanted to stone him and ultimately kill him. There were hateful things said about him, and even those most intimate to him, the disciples he loved and handpicked to be his closest friends, let him down or questioned his motives or wondered what he was thinking. Even those from his hometown, the folks he grew up around, who knew him and his mama and Joseph and the rest of the family, didn't always see him the way God saw him, the way God knew him, who he was and what he was about.

So does Jesus know our hurts? Absolutely. Is he listening, ready to understand? Yes, in a heartbeat. His heart is big enough for all our hurts.

So stop holding on to yours.

Five Ways to Let the Hurt Go Right Now

1. **Ask God to replace your hurts with his healing thoughts.** Something powerful happens when we humbly go before God, bring the hurt in our heart to him, and ask him to replace it with something else. When you're hurting, you tend to dwell on those thoughts and those feelings. But God wants more for you.

   We see what we should be thinking about in Philippians 4:8—honorable things, lovely things, commendable things, *true* things. So trade your hurts for God's thoughts. Tell God you're giving him your hurt and ask him to replace that hurt with his love. Tell God you're giving him your pain and ask him to replace that pain with his truth. Give God the loneliness you're feeling from a friend's rejection and ask God to replace that loneliness with the knowledge he is always with you. Give God your brokenness over a failed relationship and ask him to replace that brokenness with peace and wisdom to move forward. When we ask with the right motives, God hears our prayers and walks with us through the hurt to the other side.

2. **Forgive the person responsible for the hurt.** This one is difficult, especially if the person doesn't want to talk or acknowledge there's a problem. Say out loud, "Lord, I forgive [the person's name] for hurting me. Whether she realizes it or not. Whether she takes responsibility or not. I know you don't wish for me to hold on to this hurt anymore. So I forgive her. I'm letting this hurt go. Help me to never return to it."

   When you do this, remember that God doesn't put limits on forgiveness. This isn't conditional—when you forgive someone and the person does the same thing to hurt you again, this doesn't mean you get to take back your forgiveness.

Jesus said to forgive someone who sins against you "70 times seven" (Matthew 18:22). There is no expiration, no limit. That's because there's no limit with him when it comes to how many times he's willing to forgive us.

3. **Stop, pause, and pray.** Some hurts in our lives don't go away immediately. They're like tinder for a brush fire—you think the blaze has been put out only to realize later a portion was just smoldering, and not much was required to bring it back to full intensity if we're not on our guard. Forgiving hurt in our lives can be more of a process of treatment rather than an operation with immediate results, and that's why it's so important to take your hurt to Jesus the moment you sense it come up again. Tell him, "Jesus, I give this hurt to you right now. Replace it with your love. Replace it with your peace. Remind me in this moment that you are greater."

This may sound silly, but when I stop and pray like that over a hurt, the first image that comes to my mind is Jesus standing there with a fire hose, washing away those little patches of flame and white-hot coals that are threatening to relight. When we ask God for help, he responds, as the psalmist writes in Psalm 91:

> Because he is lovingly devoted to Me,
> I will deliver him;
> I will protect him because he knows My name.
> When he calls out to Me, I will answer him;
> I will be with him in trouble.
> I will rescue him and give him honor.
> (Psalm 91:14-15)

4. **Recognize that your hurt can be a stepping-stone to help others.** During one of my very first years of ministry, my team held a concert by a Christian artist for military wives in our local group and in our city. We didn't have much money

or a lot of experience, but what we lacked we made up for in prayer and a desire to see military wives ministered to. Ticket sales were low, though, and the attendance wasn't what we or the Christian artist we'd invited had hoped.

When she arrived at the venue the night of the concert, she seemed reluctant to be there, and my attempts at conversation with her didn't go very far. As a last-ditch effort to fill more seats, the artist's team had invited a local troubled-girls ministry to attend, which we'd approved. But as the concert got underway, it became clear her focus was only toward those girls. She never attempted to minister in any way to the military wives in the room whose husbands were deployed.

Though I was hurt at her lack of compassion, I knew nothing could be done about it, and resolved to just chalk it up to a lesson learned. The fit just wasn't a good one. But the lesson went further when I was copied on an email a few days later.

Someone who had attended the concert had also noticed the slight toward the military wives, and she had sent the artist a brief and polite message expressing her disappointment. The artist wrote back, copying me, with both barrels blazing. I was heartbroken and stunned, trying to wrap my head around how this artist could stand onstage just nights before, talking about Jesus, and then in this email, use such ugly and hurtful words to someone she didn't even know.

The whole situation was disappointing. But because that hurt happened for me so early on in ministry—when someone I had admired so greatly let me down so much—today I'm much more conscious of what I do in my own ministry and when I'm around other ministry leaders. I never expect to be treated a certain way. I look for ways I can encourage not just the women or the group I've been invited to speak to, but also those ministry leaders who are doing the lion's share of the work, pouring out encouragement and love on their groups. They are usually the unsung heroes, and I know their hearts well. They've got a desire to make a difference for God's kingdom, and they so want and need encouragement that they're on the right path.

What I've always told the military wives I talk with, especially when it comes to deployments, is that God can use those hurts to help us help others. We can learn from those hurts and pass on what we learn. So don't wish your hurts away or that they never happened. They've happened. Ask God to help you help someone else who is struggling right now with the same hurt.

5. **Stop worrying over your hurt.** Worry and worship can't reside in our hearts at the same time, and when we worry over our hurts, thinking about them, reliving them, fearing possibly more hurt to come, we cannot also be in a worshipful state of mind. One of my favorite scriptures is Philippians 4:6 because I am a worrier, and especially when I have hurts, I worry and agonize and they become all I focus on. But when I read this verse, I'm reminded how I'm not supposed to be anxious but thankful, and I can take any anxiousness I'm feeling to God. Let me include it here for you: "Don't worry about anything, but in everything, through prayer and petition with thanksgiving, let your requests be made known to God."

Bring to God your worries about your hurts. He has much better things for you to think about and focus on.

7

"Getting Over It" and Other Myths

Forgiveness isn't easy, is it? I haven't found it to be in my life, and I'm assuming since you're reading this, you probably haven't either. But maybe you didn't pick this up for you. Maybe you saw this title and thought of someone close to you who struggles with some things. Maybe it's things you've done, or that other people in your family or circle of friends have done, and she's moody or shows her hurt feelings or gets offended easily, and you've thought more than once, "Oh, my goodness, she just needs to get *over* it!"

We're tempted to say that, especially when we can't see the harm that's been done or the hurt in someone else's heart. But while all of us need to "get over" something so we can get on with living, it isn't as easy as flipping a switch, which sometimes that phrase implies.

Maybe we've even given this speech to ourselves: *I just need to get over her hurtful comment.* Or *I just need to get over what he did last week and stop thinking about it.* The answer to moving on from a hurtful situation isn't burying the problem or the hurt, but that's what most of us are tempted to do. As you've read, you may even have thought of shortcuts you can take when it comes to this whole forgiveness thing. Do you really need to try and have that conversation? Can't you just accept or right things that are wrong in your own heart and move on?

Forgiveness Myths

Maybe. Maybe not. So let's talk about some of the myths we fall for when it comes to forgiveness. Which ones have you tried before?

Myth: Forgiveness Should Be Easy

> When we need it, forgiveness seems like it should be an easy thing to do. But it's a whole lot harder when we're asked to give it.

When we need it, forgiveness seems like it should be an easy thing to do. But it's a whole lot harder when we're asked to give it. When you forgive, you're letting something go, and most people's tendency, our natural inclination as we've discussed, is to hold on.

I want to forgive. I want to have no record of wrongs for anyone in my life. I don't want to wake up with hurt, and I don't want to look back with regrets. I want a clean heart, a pure heart, a heart that operates from honest motives with no hidden agendas, and I want people around me to do the same.

"Can't we all just get along?" someone once asked, at the height of a raging conflict.

But we don't all get along, at least not all the time. None of us have always gotten along. Just look at poor Adam and Eve—their first argument came about because of a piece of fruit, when Eve made a decision that cost them not just the beautiful home where they were living, but altered their relationship with God and with each other. I wonder how that conversation went, as they spent their first night outside their beloved garden, now forbidden to them, sitting on opposite ends of a log, trying to stay warm by a tiny fire that Adam took *forever* to make, which might have gone quicker had Eve *just brought the right twigs and tree limbs* to begin with.

In the book of Numbers, the Israelites got tired of the manna God sent them daily. There were only so many ways you could cook up manna, and some of the Israelites had apparently seen their fill. I'm sure there were some meat-and-potato kind of men in the camp who were over the whole manna quiche and manna crepes and manna bread their wives were coming up with. They wanted something they could really put between their teeth.

When you read this in Numbers 11, you can almost see the humor (dark or not) in it. The Israelites whine and complain and fuss and fume because they've had it up to their portable George Foreman grills with the manna, and God gets very angry. Then we're told that Moses also gets angry and (maybe not thinking so clearly) takes his frustration out on God—"Why have You brought such trouble on Your servant? Why are You angry with *me*, and why do You burden me with *all these people? Did I conceive all those people? Did I give them birth…?*" (11:11-12, emphasis mine). There was a whole lot of not getting along happening right there.

Our human nature leaves us emotional. Impulsive. We're quick to judgment and slow to consideration for others. That's why we have to be taught to share when we're little. Why we have to teach our kids over and over again, to say thank you and please and not to ask for things that aren't theirs.

But when we invite Christ into our lives, we are not left with just our human nature, and we don't have to be how we were. We can remember the words we read in 2 Corinthians 5:17, "Therefore, if anyone is in Christ, there is a new creation; old things have passed away, and look, new things have come."

> When you let go of something in your heart, you make room for something brand-new.

So forgiveness isn't easy for us, but it is possible with God. And when we rely on him to help us forgive someone of their wrongs, we can anticipate the newness he will do in our own lives. When you let go of something in your heart, you make room for something brand-new.

Myth: Forgiveness Is Optional

When we buy into this myth that we don't have to forgive, we're wearing the same attitude as that of one wife who was sitting in a marriage counselor's office.

"Do you love your husband?" the counselor asked her.

"Love him?" she said, a little incredulously. "Love him? Of course, I love him!" Then she looked over at her husband. "I just don't *like* him!"

When we tell ourselves we'll just get over our hurt or irritation or frustration with someone, without forgiving that person, without saying, "I'm letting that hurt go, and I forgive what they did, and that hurt is no longer part of my thinking or part of my feelings," aren't we just putting a bandage over a scratch without adding anything to prevent it from getting infected? Sometimes scratches can heal by themselves, but they can also get worse. Sometimes they can hurt longer than they might have if we'd just added the antibacterial ointment to begin with. Sometimes, they leave scars.

So many scriptures point to forgiveness as the best choice in life, and many more don't actually mention the word *forgiveness*, but they stress the importance of not leaving hard feelings on the table.

> And be kind and compassionate to one another, forgiving one another, just as God also forgave you in Christ (Ephesians 4:32).

> Therefore, God's chosen ones, holy and loved, put on heartfelt compassion, kindness, humility, gentleness, and patience, accepting one another and forgiving one another if anyone has a complaint against another. Just as the Lord has forgiven you, so you must also forgive (Colossians 3:12-13).

> "And whenever you stand praying, if you have anything against anyone, forgive him, so that your Father in heaven will also forgive you your wrongdoing" (Mark 11:25).

God wants peace for our lives, and love in our hearts for him and for others, and how can we do that if we hold on to grudges or refuse to let hurts go and we don't forgive?

Forgiveness isn't optional. God makes it very clear in his Word that if we want his forgiveness when we mess up, we have to offer the same to others.

> Forgiveness isn't optional.

Myth: Forgiveness Requires Reconciliation

While God calls us to forgive those who hurt us, settling our differences or restoring a friendship to its original friendly condition isn't always possible. A conflict generally doesn't involve just us. Someone else is part of the equation, and their actions and choices can't be controlled or dictated by what we want to see them do. Just as we have a choice to make, so do they.

Sometimes what they choose isn't what we would choose. Or sometimes, depending on the situation, everyone involved just needs to move on.

I lost two very close friends several years ago when I held on to hurts I'd received and blown up to the size of a forest fire during our first deployment. They weren't military wives, and because of that, I examined everything they did or didn't do under the label "they just don't understand." I became hurt, and then reserved, indifferent, aloof, distant, and then just bitter. They seemed to be perfectly happy in their worlds, while mine felt in many ways like it was falling apart. Instead of accepting their friendships as they were, with what they had, my expectations were so high that no friend could have been what I was wanting.

So we stopped talking. They went their way and I went mine. When I found myself ducking out of a Target one day because I thought I saw one of them walking down an aisle, I knew I needed to get a grip. I knew I needed to let this hurt go.

So I spent a couple of days praying about it, and then I picked up the phone. I called each of them, and they were both pretty surprised to hear from me. Both had a second child by that point, and life was going well for them all (their husbands were close friends too). We caught up a little, and then I said what I'd called to say. I said I was sorry for my attitude, and I was sorry for walking away from the friendship. They'd done nothing wrong.

They both were sweet and forgiving, but things were never the same. Too much time had passed, and while we stayed somewhat connected over Facebook for a while, eventually that went away too. But there were no hard feelings. They'd forgiven me, and I'd let go of the hurt I'd held on to.

> Not every apology is going to end with a revival of a relationship.

Not every apology is going to end with a revival of a relationship. I do regret the hurt I let come between my friends and me, because I know how close they are after all these years and how much life they've done together, and I know my husband and I could have probably been part of that if I hadn't let bitterness take root. But some things can't be undone, and that's OK. You learn and you grow and you move on. I am thankful I have learned what *not* to do with friendships, and I hope that I will never repeat those feelings and attitudes with the treasured friends I have today.

Myth: Forgiveness Requires an Apology

Many of us think we can offer forgiveness to someone only if and when they ask for it. But that's not what grace is about. When it comes to forgiving someone, we've already said that a fresh start or a continued relationship won't always happen, and apologies may not happen either. Sometimes people aren't willing or they're not able. If someone who hurt you deeply dies before you ever come to a resolution, that doesn't mean you can't ever forgive.

Someone once said that a happy marriage is the union of two forgivers, and I think there's probably great truth in that for any relationship, whether that of friends or a parent and a child or a husband and a wife. Forgiving doesn't mean you'll easily forget, especially when we're talking about traumatic hurts or deep wounds. But when you forgive, when you let go of what's hurt you, when you refuse to let that hurt define you as a victim, a failure, a loser, you make room for what God wants to do.

When you extend forgiveness in your heart, whether or not someone asks for it, you gain focus, new clarity, new insight, new hope, and new purpose. You walk forward, and you do it with a new sense of the forgiveness God gives you every single day. We can forgive without someone asking for it because we recognize that what is sufficient for us is not the right behavior of someone else but the grace God gives us, recognizing that in our weakest moments, God's strength is greater, and it's by his hand we can forgive.

Myth: Forgiveness Doesn't Cost Anything

I think a lot of us go into wanting to forgive someone, or hoping to get over a situation or a hurtful circumstance, thinking it shouldn't be that hard to forgive. In our heads and our hearts, if we know Jesus, we know what he did for us; we know we're forgiven, so we should forgive others. So we get up each and every morning with the intention of forgiving that person who hurt us or who keeps saying those mean things to us. But by the end of the day, when we finally lay our heads on our pillows, looking back at how the day went, we didn't do anything that looks like forgiveness, and we may have just let the feelings get worse.

> Forgiveness *does* cost something.

I think this happens because we don't recognize that forgiveness *does* cost something. Or maybe we do realize it—and that's why we don't forgive easily, because we're not willing to pay the price.

Forgiving your husband for emotional or physical betrayal is costly. Forgiving a relative or a parent of sexual or physical or emotional abuse costs something. Forgiving a coworker who blamed you for their mistake, with serious consequences, can cost you. Forgiving people who abandoned you during your divorce or during your rehab or during treatment for your disease comes with a price. The cost is costly. The cost is part of you.

First, forgiveness costs you your claim for justice. Your right to restitution. Repayment. Compensation, emotional or otherwise. When you forgive, you're saying that person doesn't owe you. Anything.

Second, forgiveness costs you part of yourself. When I think about forgiveness, I think of the sacrifice involved. You're giving up your claim for justice; you're also giving up the need to be right. Like a soldier who selflessly throws himself on a live grenade for his fellow troops, absorbing the impact of the blast so they don't have to, that's what happens when we forgive. We absorb what's been done, we fold ourselves over the wrong, we cover over the hurt, but we don't do it on our own and we don't hold on to it ourselves. We release it to God, and he takes it, along with all the wrongs that we ourselves are responsible for.

> Forgiveness costs. But what we receive in place of what's given far outweighs the price.

So, yes, forgiveness costs. But what we receive in place of what's given far outweighs the price.

Lay It Down

I've shared a lot of stories with you about times in my life when I've struggled with hurts. The danger with that in a book about forgiveness, and in such a limited amount of space, is that I can quickly start sounding like I've got bitter grapes or I'm just whining or I have unresolved issues that need some serious examining. You may be thinking even now, *Good grief, girlfriend, find a therapist!*

But the reason I can even share those stories with you is because of the change God's placed in me with those hurts. I know there is someone reading this right now who needs to know they're not alone in their hurts, and that there is healing when they forgive, there is change that can be discovered, because that is what I've experienced.

Hurts don't all look the same. What's hurtful for you may not be hurtful for me, but they're still legitimate hurts. I'll hear from friends whose husbands are traveling for work and are gone for three days, and they feel like they're losing their minds. Then they look at me and feel bad because my husband is away for his third deployment, and they're thinking, *How can I be whining about three days when someone else is struggling with ten months?*

But here's a secret—military wives do the exact same thing to each other. The air force wife apologizes to the navy wife because her air force husband's deployment is only six months, the navy wife apologizes to the army wife because her navy husband's tour is only seven to ten months, and the army wife apologizes to her army wife friend because hers was only a year without an extension, unlike what happened to her friend. My goodness! This is one area we really need to lay off the apologies. We've all got hurts, so let's help each other move past our hurts. We don't always have to compare. We don't have to play the Who Has It Worse game. Hurts are hurts.

Can we just agree here that your perspective is your perspective, and your experience informs your perspective? Certainly, we can gain a new sense of it when we see what other people go through, and we realize that maybe some things we tend to get upset over aren't really so big in the bigger scheme of things. But if something has wounded you—whether you're being oversensitive or not—your hurt is still your hurt. You may need to work through something that another friend can

> Work through your hurt. Forgive in your time and with God's leading.

just let roll off her back and not give a second thought (and thinks you should do the same).

Work through your hurt. Forgive in your time and with God's leading. (And don't worry about what's-her-name.)

One of the ways God has taught me about forgiveness and letting go and surrendering to him in the purest of terms is what he's shown me in my marriage over the last few years. You can't be married without eventually experiencing some type of conflict. Money, they say, is the topic couples argue most about. Sex is probably another one. Family might be another—your parents, his parents, your kids—negotiating that ever-changing formula for helping everyone get along and stay on their best behavior.

But do you know what I think is the core issue of most marriage struggles? If we could solve this issue, I believe 99.9 percent of our problems and arguments in marriage might go away.

Selfishness.

I want my way and not his. I want *him* to want my way and not his. I want him to see me as right, all the time and not just occasionally. I want him to meet my needs. I want, I want, I want. For him to read my mind. For him to take care of me. For him to give me what I want. Boy, can a girl want things. (So can guys.)

I didn't marry my husband because he's exactly like me. I married him because he wasn't like me, because he looked at things a little differently, and I liked his perspective on life. I liked that he could make me laugh when I wanted to cry, and he made life special for just being in mine. But as the years have gone by, I still notice that I try my very best to change him to be more like me.

Maybe you have no idea what I'm talking about.

But I have a sneaky suspicion that you do.

As God walked me through some experiences I've written about in other books—lessons I learned from the Proverbs 31 wife and that controversial word *submission* that we find in Ephesians 5 among other passages in the Bible—he didn't just deal with me in my attitude on marriage. He taught me a really important lesson about my attitude toward him.

Before I can even think about whether I'm putting myself or my husband first in my marriage, I need to just think about my life and whether I'm following God—or running out in front of him, trying my best to lead.

Am I submitting my life to God? Am I willingly obeying him?

> Am I submitting my life to God? Am I willingly obeying him?

Or am I not?

Our ongoing battle is a battle of will—do I insist on winning or do I recognize God already has won? That choice spills over into my choices and decisions and attitudes in all of my relationships. Do I put myself first? Or do I put God first?

James touches on the source of these conflicts that come up so often in our lives, because they came up in the early church too. Christians were fighting among each other, physically divided, drawing lines, and holding on to what James calls "cravings that are at war within you" (James 4:1). People were determined to achieve pleasures, things they believed would make themselves happy, instead of uniting to follow one common purpose of serving God.

> You desire and do not have. You murder and covet and cannot obtain. You fight and war. You do not have because you do not ask. You ask and don't receive because you ask with wrong motives, so that you may spend it on your evil desires (James 4:2-3).

You desire and do not have. Some days I just long for a time when all of us will be happy with our own lives, with where God places us and how he's using us, and we are all too busy making sure we're following his instructions to be concerned about everyone else and what

> Too many of us worry about what others have that we don't or what we have that others don't.

they're doing or not doing. Too many of us worry about what others have that we don't or what we have that others don't. Or we worry if someone else's dreams don't look exactly like ours, and maybe there's something wrong with that person, or worse, maybe there's something wrong with us.

But maybe with age comes a little bit more wisdom or maturity. I've found as I've had a few more birthdays (and I have more things I have to do and I'm responsible for) that I cannot do everything. I don't have the gifts or talents to do it all. I don't have the wisdom and intelligence to understand it all. I don't have the time, patience, and fortitude to do everything. And when I say everything, I mean anything I see other people doing and the thought crosses my mind, *Shouldn't I be doing that?*

No! Not necessarily.

There is plenty of work for everyone. There is plenty of happiness for everyone. There is plenty of God's glory for everyone.

Oh, my friend, if we could just be satisfied with that.

Think about the kind of joy we might have in life, the ease we might experience with forgiveness, if we could just be satisfied with *him.*

You do not have because you do not ask or *you ask with wrong motives.* How many times do we get our britches in a bind because we assume someone's answer or response instead of simply asking and waiting for their reply? Or we ask but we ask with a hidden agenda or a manipulative motive behind our request?

> There is deep satisfaction that comes when we get over one specific thing: ourselves.

There is deep satisfaction that comes when we get over one specific thing: ourselves. When we stop giving in to this need we have to look out for number one, and we start just giving everything over to Jesus. Because God always wins. We can't outdo him. We can't out give him. He wins. So which side do we choose? Our side, or his?

Steps to Overcoming Discord

James has some pretty clear instructions for the church and how they need to handle the conflicts that have arisen. He doesn't say, "This group over here needs to acknowledge that this other group is right." He doesn't say, "You people just need to talk this thing out. I'm sending peer mediators over there right now."

No, James doesn't hold an intervention. He gives specific steps they need to take to overcome the discord among themselves, to rid the conflict in their hearts and with each other once and for all. These are good steps for us as well.

1. Submit to God (v. 7)

We don't like this word. We don't like saying it in relationship to other people, and if we're honest, we don't always feel comfortable saying it about our relationship with God, the one who created us, who made us, who gave us breath and life. This idea of yielding our will doesn't sit well in our "be all that you can be," "fake it till you make it," "kick down doors and take names" culture.

If you grew up in a home with parents or others who were ugly toward you, or who dominated you by fear or controlled you with threats of how much God would hate you if you didn't do what they wanted you to do, you may struggle with this idea of submission to God. Your only example of authority gave you a completely wrong sense of who God is. I pray you take time to study and read about the love God has for his children, the love he has for you. He wants the best for us, and because of that, he asks us to trust him enough to follow him with every part of our lives.

> Do you want to know the secret to being able to forgive? Learn how to submit your will to God.

Yes, he wants our love. But he also wants our obedience, and that's what submission is. Do you want to know the secret to being able to forgive? Learn how to submit your will to God. Discipline yourself, teach yourself, develop the habit of giving over to God everything you would prefer to hold on to, and trust God enough with the outcomes.

When I struggle with this, and I recognize that I'm struggling, one of the little prayers I whisper is "I trust you, Jesus." I don't know what will happen today or what will happen tomorrow or next year, but I know he walks with me every moment and step of the way. He's walking with you too.

2. Resist the devil (v. 7)

James offers several commands here that contain a promise, and it starts with this one. If you do *this*, then *this* will happen. If you resist the devil, then he will flee from you. Submission to God is our goal, but plenty of distractions are thrown at us and attempts to convince us we just need to do what we want to do. Don't buy in to it. I know how tempting it is to talk and keep talking about a situation that has hurt you. But don't do it. Don't let that temptation suck you down into a pit of no mercy, no grace, and no life.

God's Word doesn't say the devil will leave you alone and *then* you can resist him. No, we have to firmly plant ourselves with God, knowing that as soon as we do, Satan can't do anything about it. So stop the gossip. Stop the nitpicking. Stop the rehashing over and over of what's been done to you. You have other things God has called you to do.

3. Draw near to God (v. 8)

"Draw near to God, and He will draw near to you." So we step away from the enemy and we step close to experience God's presence. Only by spending time with God and his wisdom, his goodness, his way to handle a conflict or problem, can we truly figure out how to forgive and let go. This means time in his Word. This means when you find yourself frustrated or feeling defeated, like the hurt is too big for you to overcome, you reach out to God and you ask him to draw near. You ask him for his help, for his understanding, for his ability to give grace. This is how we overcome conflict.

4. Cleanse your hands and purify your hearts (v. 8b)

In other words, start over. Resolve to stop letting hurt keep you in its grip. As tempting as it is to make sarcastic comments or remarks toward someone you're having a problem with, don't do it. Make the choice to change yourself. Clean out all the junk in your heart and mind about that person or that situation you need to forgive. Let it go, and don't let it come back.

> Clean out all the junk in your heart and mind about that person or that situation you need to forgive.

5. Be miserable (v. 9)

This verse might look odd—in order to forgive, I have to be miserable? Aren't I already miserable with what's happened? I thought forgiveness was supposed to make me feel better?

What James says here is we need to recognize the wrong we've done, even if it's just that we've allowed hurt to build up and turn into resentment or anger or strong dislike. We should be mindful of and convicted over our sin, because when we're reminded of the things we've done that did not deserve God's grace and yet he gave it, we should be able to offer grace and forgiveness toward someone else.

6. Humble yourself (v. 10)

"Humble yourselves before the Lord, and He will exalt you." When you study the life of Jesus, what he did and how he did it, you quickly realize he never defended himself when people attacked him. He didn't protest insults or return the name-calling. He didn't go after those who didn't agree with him. Even when he was falsely accused and misunderstood by the common people and by the religious leaders and by the government officials, he never defended himself. He defended God. He got angry for God when people had turned his holy place, the temple, into a profitable business instead of a place of worship (Matthew 21). But he never got angry or self-righteous or offended for himself.

When we can humble ourselves before God, we can let go of our hurts and offenses, knowing that our joy, our sense of well-being, is with him and not with other people.

But here is where we lay it all down, where we get into the nitty-gritty of what it means to submit to God. James just makes it very clear: "It is a sin for the person who knows to do what is good and doesn't do it" (v. 17).

Ouch. Can't really explain that one away, can we? We know God's Word says to forgive. To not hold grudges. To let hurts and slights and offenses go. So what does it mean when we don't? We're not doing what he's called us to do. So, if we refuse to forgive, we are the ones who are offending. If we refuse to forgive, we are the ones who are being the jerks, the ones who have deemed ourselves more important than others—or even more important than God.

> People are going to hurt you, intentionally or accidentally. So what are you going to do about it?

Conflicts are going to happen. Problems are going to come up. People are going to hurt you, intentionally or accidentally. So what are you going to do about it?

Do you know what Isaac did about it? Remember Isaac? We find part of his story in Genesis 26. He was the son of Abraham, the son God had promised and his parents had waited a lifetime for. He in turn became a dad, whose sons (Jacob and Esau) couldn't get along. He also made mistakes similar to those of his father. At one point, living in a foreign land, he declared that his wife was his sister so he wouldn't be killed for her, and his lie was exposed. But God still continued to bless Isaac and made him very wealthy.

Others around Isaac resented his success, were envious of his blessings, and did everything they could to make life hard. They stopped up the wells Abraham had dug, and Isaac was forced to move his many herds and livestock not once but three times because of the quarrels that erupted with the local herdsmen when he tried to settle down in a spot. His servants dug a well in one area, which sparked an argument over who had rights to the water, and Isaac named it Quarrel. He moved on and dug another well, where they still complained and fought, and Isaac named that well Hostility. But finally, in the last place he stopped, there were no more arguments, no one standing around to pick a fight, and Isaac named the place Open Spaces because God had "made room" for them (Genesis 26:22).

I've thought a lot about Isaac's story and the open spaces he found when he kept on looking. Isn't that what we need to do? Instead of hunkering down, declaring war, and refusing to budge until our rights are recognized— what if we just moved on? What if we let that place go, left it to those unhappy people and just kept going, looking for the open space God has for us and the freedom we experience when we truly practice forgiveness?

> Sometimes God also removes you from that place of conflict and negativity and hurt for your protection. Don't go back.

I saw a quote the other day attributed to Rick Warren: "God sometimes removes a person from your life for your protection. Don't run after them." I would add that sometimes God also removes you from that place of conflict and negativity and hurt for your protection. Don't go back.

Five Truths about Forgiveness
You Can Know Right Now

1. **Forgiveness is possible with God's help.** God loves to help us come back to him, and when we are dealing with a hurt that brings up pain and resentment and any number of other negative emotions, we are inching or sometimes leaping away from him. But forgiving someone will never keep us at arm's length from God; our forgiving actions will only bring us closer to him. God helps us move forward and stop looking back. Trust that you can follow him. Trust he will help you forgive.

2. **God expects us to forgive.** This has no room for negotiation, friends. God wants us to forgive. He wants us to forgive our enemies who do us wrong, forgive our friends who say careless things, forgive our family members who make us want to cry or tear our hair out. He wants us to let it go, and he expects us to do it. Jesus said in Luke 6:37, "Do not judge, and you will not be judged. Do not condemn, and you will not be condemned. Forgive, and you will be forgiven."

3. **Forgiveness restores a right relationship with God.** We do not have to have an ongoing relationship with someone to forgive that person. But we still need to forgive, because how we treat that person impacts how we respond to God's leading in our lives.

4. **True forgiveness releases hard feelings.** The person you need to forgive may never offer an apology or admit any wrongdoing. But your forgiveness for their wrong releases those feelings that keep you from walking forward, maybe even from starting a new friendship or pouring into your

current relationships because you're afraid or because you now have great doubt and mistrust of other people.

Other emotions could be holding you back from the plan God has for you. When we hold kindness and compassion in our hearts (Ephesians 4:32), it's difficult to hold anger and cynicism at the same time. Get rid of the junky feelings—get rid of those negative emotions that come when we refuse to forgive someone. Give the forgiveness, breathe in God's grace, and let that grace shine out to others.

5. **Forgiveness means losing yourself and gaining more of God's presence and love in your life.** I think about Jesus's words in Matthew 5, when he talks about going the extra mile in his name:

> "If anyone slaps you on your right cheek, turn the other to him also."

> "If anyone forces you to go one mile, go with him two."

> "Give to the one who asks you, and don't turn away from the one who wants to borrow from you."

These are not easy statements to follow! These instructions go against everything in our culture today. But Jesus has a reason and a purpose in what he says. He points out that if we love just those who are easy to love, what does that mean? Does that make us any more right than people who do wrong? Look at his words:

> "If you do what is good to those who are good to you, what credit is that to you? Even sinners do that...But love your enemies, do what is good, and lend, expecting nothing in return. Then your reward will be great, and you will be sons of the Most High" (Luke 6:33,35).

Forgiveness isn't all about us. We forgive because we recognize God forgives us. We give grace because we understand that God is gracious with us.

This is simple to hear but not so simple to carry out each and every day. Yet, we also know God gives us strength to do what's hard. And when it feels like the impossible, that's when we can count on God the most.

8

Forgiving Yourself

In the experiences of a person's life, I wonder if childhood is perhaps the most special time. When you're a kid, you don't think so much about the impact of your choices and decisions as you do when you're older. You just live, and live out loud. There aren't so many shades of uncertainty, at least there's not supposed to be. When you're a kid, you just play. You just laugh. You might cry, but you also love—willingly and unconditionally in most respects. You haven't been taught yet to apply the conditions so many of us have in place by the time we're adults.

Now that I'm well into my thirties, I can look back at my twenties and shake my head a little at what a freight train I was. I was so determined to achieve and accomplish and pursue—much of it in honorable pursuit of God.

I wanted to live large for Christ, and I used *pursue* a lot in my vocabulary back then. I pursued Christ. I was so intent to make a difference for him, I spent a lot of energy and time and effort running after him.

But I've realized something the last few years that I knew but refused to recognize.

He was already standing next to me.

Can you see it? How hard we often work to be better than we are? The books we read, the Bible studies we sign up for? We try so intensely sometimes to see a difference or make a difference, and we do it all for a smile from our Savior, or a pat on the back or some strong indication, perhaps a blessing, that God is happy with us.

If we would just turn our heads slightly to the right, we'd see him standing right next to us.

So there we are, on our invisible treadmills going full speed through life, sweat pouring from our faces, struggling to breathe, looking out in front of us trying to get a glimpse of Jesus. If we would just turn our heads slightly to the right, we'd see him standing right next to us. And maybe we'd wonder why we were running.

There is nothing wrong with passion and excitement and fostering a strong desire to live out God's instructions or call on our lives. There's nothing wrong with growing in God's Word and making time for Bible study. We need to do those things. But too often we let that passion propel us past God's call into something of our own making. Duty. Check boxes. To-do lists not necessarily from God. That, I think, is when we can get into trouble, and when we can make mistakes and form regrets.

Because looking back at those energetic twenties, some of what I did was what God called me to do, and some of it, if I'm honest, was just for me. I did things back then that if I could, I would have done differently, like the scattered path of friendships I dropped like rocks on the ground every time my family moved away. By the time I reached high school, I was in my tenth school and fourth state, and that pattern of moving on stayed with me well into college and adulthood. I didn't stay connected, and as a result, I don't have many of those close friendships forged over time and over the good and bad that so many others have.

I have other regrets I've shared before. My son is now a teenager, and it makes me a little sad when I think about the things I could have done differently with him when he was younger, the time I could have taken and didn't, the moments I wished away instead of embracing. There are still days when I struggle with spending time with him and doing things for our family or spending time in ministry, encouraging other women in their relationships with God. Sometimes I wish for a do-over. I'm sure I'm not the only parent who feels that way.

You probably have your own regrets. As a teenager, or a young adult in your early twenties, you made choices that impact your life today. You've made decisions that have hurt you or your family financially or emotionally. Something you did hurt someone close to you, and the healing and forgiveness still haven't come, and you wish you'd never done it. Or maybe someone did something to you that wasn't your fault, wasn't your responsibility, and yet you still blame yourself for letting it happen.

> Something you did hurt someone close to you, and the healing and forgiveness still haven't come.

Convicted or Condemned

I don't know about you, but I can feel guilty sometimes just walking out of a grocery store. It's silly—I haven't done anything wrong, I'm taking nothing with me I haven't paid for, but I will still hold my breath as I step through the door, wondering if some alarm is about to go off proclaiming to everyone that I'm a criminal.

I think a lot of us walk around feeling this way sometimes and don't even realize it. I have a sweet friend who is always worried about how her actions might hurt someone else's feelings. She is hypersensitive about doing the right thing at all times and stresses when she thinks she hasn't. Another friend, a single mom, worries about her kids when she's at work and worries about work when she's home with her kids. She's always wondering whether she's done the right thing. Another friend wrestles with a marriage that's severely struggling. Her husband has told her he doesn't love her anymore and is only staying until the kids are grown before he leaves her. Somehow, she keeps thinking, she's done something to make him not love her anymore, and yet she's tried everything she can think of to show him her love.

At a conference I spoke at, a mom came up to me with tears in her eyes and shared with me the great amount of guilt she felt after learning her child was sexually abused by a relative. She was mortified she hadn't recognized what was happening sooner, and she was beating herself up daily for not doing whatever might have prevented her child from being hurt. The guilt she felt was unbearable, but she was taking each day to trust God to help her through the hurt, as well as trusting him to walk with her as she helped her child.

> There's a difference in the conviction God gives us when he wants our attention over something we need to change, and in the condemnation we put on ourselves.

There's a difference in the conviction God gives us when he wants our attention over something we need to change, and in the condemnation we put on ourselves. If there's a white noise we listen to that drowns out God's truth when it comes to our forgiveness of ourselves, this is it. We condemn ourselves when we mess up, and we believe we can never make it right or make it better or change. We condemn ourselves when we're not responsible for someone else's actions but we convince ourselves that we are. We condemn ourselves when we buy into the lie that we've made too many mistakes or harbored too many hard feelings for God to love us or see us or want to hear from us. But that's wrong.

Romans 8 tells us there is no condemnation over us when we have a relationship with Christ "because the Spirit's law of life in Christ Jesus has set you free from the law of sin and of death" (Romans 8:2).

No condemnation means God doesn't hold on to our faults. That's why he sent his Son, to set us free to live a free life. We don't have to hold on to our faults either.

I think we understand what that means, especially if we know, deep down, we haven't done anything wrong, when we are confusing worry and stress for guilt and blame. We know there is freedom when we walk with Christ versus when we don't. We should feel any weight of guilt lifted when we make a habit of giving those worries or problems to God every day. But it isn't easy to let go of the guilt. It's not easy to let go of the resentment and blame we're so tempted to hold on to, even when we're not sure we've done anything to deserve it.

But what about when we have actually done something wrong? When we have made mistakes we regret? Or choices or decisions that we know now we shouldn't have chosen?

How do we forgive ourselves?

There is a lot of talk these days about "self-love" and accepting yourself "just the way you are." Spiritual gurus who have no connection to God but massive followings have convinced people they don't need God in their lives to feel forgiven—they just have to forgive themselves. This is a dangerous line to walk when we think we just have to love ourselves to be happy. This is wrong, because our love can go only so far. But God's love never quits.

> God does not bless a perfect woman—he blesses the woman who recognizes her imperfections and trusts him to use her anyway.

I love how the Message words Psalm 136 because it's such a strong reminder that God doesn't quit, even when we want to quit on ourselves. Read the entire passage on your own, but look at these last few verses:

> God remembered us when we were down,
> *His love never quits.*
> Rescued us from the trampling boot,
> *His love never quits.*
> Takes care of everyone in time of need.
> *His love never quits.*

Thank God, who did it all!
His love never quits!

If God refuses to quit on you, then how can you quit on yourself? That's what you're doing when you refuse to forgive yourself, when you hold grudges against yourself, when you won't give yourself a break or permission to be anything less than perfect and you beat yourself up when you're not. But God does not bless a perfect woman—he blesses the woman who recognizes her imperfections and trusts him to use her anyway.

Of course, we need to recognize when we've made mistakes and to confess those mistakes to God. We create a problem, though, when we ask for God's forgiveness and we're unwilling to forgive ourselves. We resent the mistakes we've made, or the actions we took that led to bad results or negative consequences, and almost like our own personal punishment, we hold those feelings in. Every time something happens that reminds us of our mistake, we point it out to ourselves: "See? Remember what you did? Remember how you failed? Remember why you're so unhappy?" The cycle just keeps going if we don't put a stop to it. The noise just keeps rumbling.

> I cannot do anything without the help of God.

What has helped me the most when I've needed to forgive myself is to recognize first that I cannot do anything without the help of God. I hold tight to Romans 8:28—"We know that all things work together for the good of those who love God: those who are called according to His purpose." When I'm questioning what God is doing, and wondering sometimes how my circumstances or my situation can be anything but good, this verse reminds me over and over that God always works for my good, and even when I can't see it, he is moving in ways that will glorify him and benefit me. I may not see direct blessings, but I know I will see his blessing on my life as a whole.

This verse also comes with a condition, though. God works for the good of those who love him, and it's only those who love God who are called to do his will, to carry out his purpose, who will be used in ways he envisions that we might not.

We are not the first to struggle with making mistakes. Even those who desire to follow God with everything they have still sometimes come up short. I wonder how Moses felt spending so much time with God, eagerly listening and accepting his commands for the Israelites, only to come back down the mountain to share what God had said and finding that the people had completely abandoned God by worshipping a golden calf. We know that Moses got so mad he threw down the tablets, completely destroying them. He was angry, he was frustrated, and I'm sure a part of him wanted to see God give the Israelites exactly what they deserved.

God did punish the offending Israelites, but he did not wipe them out as he'd threatened. He also reminded Moses and the Israelites just who he was—"a compassionate and gracious God, slow to anger and rich in faithful love and truth" (Exodus 34:6).

I love what Moses says to God in verse 9. "My Lord…please go with us. Even though this is a stiff-necked people, forgive our wrongdoing and sin, and accept us as Your own possession." Notice Moses never makes excuses for the people, or promises that they'll do better, or that their behavior will improve in any way. Instead, Moses makes it clear he and the others are relying on God's forgiveness, his faithfulness, and his favor.

That's something we have to do when we're figuring out how to forgive ourselves.

Remember His Forgiveness

God gives us second chances again and again. He forgives us where we fail him. He restores us and brings us back to where he needs us to be. I think about Jonah and the lesson he learned after his intentional choice to run from God and not obey him when God asked him to go to Nineveh. By the time he reached the belly of the huge fish, I believe his remorse was real as he shared in his prayer:

> Those who cling to worthless idols
> forsake faithful love,
> but as for me, I will sacrifice to You
> with a voice of thanksgiving.
> I will fulfill what I have vowed.
> Salvation is from the LORD!
> (Jonah 2:8-9)

But Jonah's story doesn't end there. He did what God asked him to do. He went to Nineveh and shared the message God told him to deliver—that they would be destroyed if they didn't repent. That's when the miraculous happened. A city known for such evil, such violence, such horrible hearts and terrible activities, turned to God. They repented. They were brought to their knees with such a simple statement from Jonah, but a statement infused with the power of God's Spirit, and they recognized God as their authority and acknowledged the wrong they had done.

You might think after reading about Jonah's remorse as he sat in the dark dank stomach of a fish that he would have been ecstatic and joyful and excited that a portion of God's children had returned to him. But read Jonah 4 and his reaction:

> But Jonah was greatly displeased and became furious. He prayed to the LORD: "Please, LORD, isn't this what I said while I was still in my own country? That's why I fled toward Tarshish in the first place. I knew that You are a merciful and compassionate God, slow to become angry, rich in faithful love, and One who relents from sending disaster. And now, LORD, please take my life from me, for it is better for me to die than to live" (Jonah 4:1-3).

Do you notice it, after our time together so far? Can you recognize the white noise of resentment and anger surrounding Jonah, the only party pooper at God's celebration welcoming the Ninevites home, like the older brother at the father's party for the prodigal son, thinking, *Why should he get any blessing? Why should he be given any second chances?*

Like the slave who ignored the grace his master gave him, Jonah forgot the grace and forgiveness and second chance God gave him. We do the same when it comes to our own forgiveness. We can refuse to forgive ourselves with the same stubbornness and self-righteousness Jonah displayed toward the Ninevites. All that does, though, is drive a wedge between us and God because we already know God forgives. He wants to restore us to full relationship with him. But when we refuse to forgive ourselves, we hold on to regret and disappointment that keeps us from completely realizing the wholeness God can bring us back to when we forgive.

> God has greater plans for you, but you can't move forward into his purpose for your life when you cling to punishments of your own making.

If you are struggling with forgiving yourself today for a situation where you made a mistake, or you just flat out chose wrong over right, can I encourage you to just let it go? God has greater plans for you, but you can't move forward into his purpose for your life when you cling to punishments of your own making for your mistakes or sin that God wants to forgive. If you've confessed your actions to God, if you've sincerely asked him to forgive you, then it is also time to forgive yourself. He's already forgiven you because he has compassion for those who recognize his authority, and we can be confident that, as the psalmist says, he has exonerated or removed our sin and our mistakes "as far as the east is from the west."

So if God, who is Almighty, who is the Creator of the universe, is willing to forgive you and offer grace and compassion to you, it's time to offer it to yourself.

Remember His Faithfulness

If you think about it, you can reflect on various seasons of your life and see God's fingerprints touching and surrounding you. He is always faithful toward us; we are the ones who specialize in inconsistencies.

One of the most beautiful descriptions of God we find in several places in the Bible is about his compassion and faithfulness. Jonah even mentioned it, though it's ironic that he did it in the form of a complaint. And David said of him:

> The LORD is compassionate and gracious,
> slow to anger and rich in faithful love.
> (Psalm 103:8)

David, a man who loved the Lord, a man after God's own heart (1 Samuel 13:14), who was anointed as king of Israel, God's chosen, still did not always do what was right. Though he was fiercely committed to the Lord, he also had weaknesses. The one most people know about is his affair with Bathsheba, but that wasn't the only failure David had to cope with. He mistakenly carried out a census, counting and recording the number of troops under his command, which perhaps implied he was more focused on his own strength and force than on his desire to trust God to continue leading and protecting the people. As a dad, he wasn't always attentive or responsible when it came to his children. His son Solomon went on to become one of the greatest kings in Israel's history, but another son, Absalom, brought disaster and misfortune.

> God showed his faithfulness to David, correcting and disciplining him when his actions called for it, but never withholding his love.

Those times in David's life where he went

one way when he should have gone the other—when he made a wrong choice instead of doing what was right—could have ended his relationship with the Lord, or at least ended God's blessing on him. But that's not what happened. God never abandoned David. He showed his faithfulness to David, correcting and disciplining him when his actions called for it, but never withholding his love.

When it's difficult to forgive yourself, when you feel like a failure and you wonder if you can ever possibly make things right, remember God's faithfulness and what he has already done for you and with you up to this point.

If you worry that you will keep making the same mistake, if you find you're always asking forgiveness of God for the same sins or wrongdoing—and it's getting harder to forgive yourself because you feel so weak and you wonder why you just can't get it together—remember God's faithfulness and hold on to 1 Corinthians 10:13—"No temptation has overtaken you except what is common to humanity. God is faithful, and He will not allow you to be tempted beyond what you are able, but with the temptation He will also provide a way of escape so that you are able to bear it."

Remember His Favor

God uses difficult moments to teach us and correct us, but also to remind us that life is just better when we put him first. This doesn't mean we suddenly have an easy button where everything goes smoothly when we push it. But when we do walk through the hard stuff, we don't have to walk alone.

When forgiveness for yourself doesn't come right away, ask God to show you his favor as you look for ways to make changes in your life to correct the course of what you have done. Proverbs 11:27 tells us:

> The one who searches for what is good finds favor,
> but if someone looks for trouble, it will come to him.

So often our thoughts and feelings can either help us move

forward or hold us in place. When we're stuck, unable to move forward because we can't forgive ourselves, sometimes we have to be intentional with our thoughts, recognizing that what we think has a direct impact on how we feel, which impacts our choices and decisions going forward. So apply Philippians 4:8 with intention and with fervor. Think about the good things in your life, and if you have trouble doing that, start with the good things about God. When we refuse to forgive ourselves, we are essentially digging a pit and falling into a hole of our own making (Psalm 7:15-16), but God wants more for you.

God wants more for us all.

Five Ways to Forgive Yourself Now

1. **Write a letter to God.** Tell him everything you're struggling with and why you're finding it hard to forgive yourself. Then read these scriptures and tell God why you know he's already forgiven you: 1 John 1:9; Isaiah 43:25; 2 Chronicles 7:14; and Proverbs 28:13.

   Pray and ask God to help you forgive yourself. You may find it helpful to tear up or burn the letter after you've prayed. As you see the letter vanish, understand that God has also forgiven and removed your sin. You can freely forgive yourself because there's nothing left to hold on to.

2. **Focus on what's good in your life.** We often let the negative far outweigh everything else that's wonderful. When in a state of unforgiveness, it's easy to see everything with a gloomy cast or tint to it. But there are blessings in your life right now that God wants you to see and remember. What about your kids? What about your spouse? What about the work you do or the volunteering or ministry you're part of in your church or community? What about the friends who have stood by you, especially during the hard times?

   Make a list of those blessings or a list of what you're grateful for, and read that list daily so you can start seeing the good that's in your life and not just the bad. Ask God to help you see his little blessings each day and make a choice to look intentionally for them and be grateful.

3. **Let go a little bit each day.** Just as forgiving someone else can be a process and not happen immediately, the same can be said when it's about forgiving yourself. Give yourself time—but don't stop being intentional. Each day ask God to heal your heart a little more, and each day allow yourself less and less time to focus on what went wrong.

4. **Believe today is a new day, full of promise and of hope.** We have hope because of the promise Christ fulfilled for us. Think about the day after his crucifixion and what that must have been like for the people who loved and followed him. But what about the next day? When Jesus came out of that tomb, he brought with him hope for the world. We can hope for nothing greater than a relationship and eternity with him. Everything else pales in comparison. We have hope because of Christ. We have second chances because of the gift of God's Son to us all.

5. **Focus on growing into the person God wants you to become.** We hear often that God loves us just the way we are, and I believe that's true. He loves us and asks us to come to him, just as we are. Broken, banged up, or bruised. But I don't believe he wants us to stay exactly how we start. That's because all of us are born sinners (Romans 3:23) in need of a relationship with God, who saves us and who loves us and who wants us to become more like him.

Peter ends his second letter with these words: "Therefore, dear friends, since you know this in advance, be on your guard, so that you are not led away by the error of lawless people and fall from your own stability. But *grow* in the grace and knowledge of our Lord and Savior Jesus Christ" (2 Peter 3:17-18a, emphasis mine). Learning to forgive—others as well as ourselves—brings us that much closer to him.

9

When You're Mad at God

We sat in the quiet of the church sanctuary, two chairs pulled together, our knees almost touching, listening to the faint laughter and conversation in the hall behind us as women lined up during the lunch break. Just a little while before, as I was speaking to the group, I saw her tears fall and thought she might need some more time just to talk. Just to be. Just to say out loud whatever was bothering her. Sometimes as a wife and a mom, you don't always get that opportunity.

She started telling me about her kids. Her son was nine with muscular dystrophy. He was starting to have enough difficulty walking that they knew he probably needed to start using a wheelchair soon. Her daughter, a little younger, had autism. This young mom sat in front of me, looking helpless and tired and worn down and much older than her actual age. As her tears fell and she wiped her nose with a tissue, she assured me over and over how much she loved her kids. But then she took a breath and looked at me, ready to unload what I'm sure was on her heart during that morning's session.

"I love my kids. But I'm not sure if I love God anymore," she said. "I don't understand how he could allow these things to happen to my kids. They're *kids*. They're innocent. Neither one of them will ever have the chance to just be normal. My son may not even grow up to be an adult." She paused. "What did they do to deserve these lives they've been given?" Her lip trembled.

"I'm so mad at him," she said. "I stopped praying a long time ago, because he didn't seem to answer anything I asked. Why would God do this? Why would he do this to children? Why would he do this to my husband and me?"

> "Why would God do this to children? Why would he do this to my husband and me?"

Things happen in our lives, hurts and disappointments and tragedies we can't explain and don't understand. If you're not a Christian and you don't have that relationship with Christ, you might be prone to say God is out to get you. But if you are a Christian and you do know Christ and his love and you strive to follow him and live for him, you may not want to say God is out to get you out loud, but you secretly may still wonder deep down if he is—or at least you question what he's thinking.

If you'd talked to me before I started working on this book, I would have told you I'd never had a moment in my life where I got mad at God for something, angry enough with him that I didn't want to talk with him. I've always tried to believe that Romans 8:28 holds true—that God works for our good even in the toughest stuff we've been through, like three years of unemployment or the time an author I was collaborating with broke our contract after I'd already completed her book. I also have never had a child or a close family member go through the debilitating and ravaging harm of a terminal disease.

But that was before my husband didn't get to come home.

Cliff has deployed three times in the last six years. That's thirty months out of the last seventy-two, which means he's been gone more than 40 percent of the time. Like a lot of military families, the weariness of being apart weighs on you. You don't take being together for granted, ever, and being apart doesn't get easier. Third time is *not* a charm when it comes to deployment, in case you were wondering. You don't get used to being away from your spouse, you just learn to cope better. I've seen that with our family.

Each deployment is different. Our life seasons have been different. Caleb was six the first time, nine the second time, and he's become a teenager while his dad's been gone this round. Each deployment has found us in a different location, sometimes with family around, sometimes without. There were times in past deployments I felt distant from God, but there were also moments and months I felt my absolute closest to him. I can definitely say that about this most recent one. Maybe I learned from the last two, maybe it's a little more spiritual maturity, a deeper understanding of God's truth, but whatever the reason, I am grateful for his strength and help in persevering when things get hard.

Even with God's strength under me and around me for so many months, though, part of me just misses my husband. Being apart when you're married isn't normal. So when Cliff started mentioning the possibility his battalion might come home from Afghanistan earlier than originally thought, I couldn't help but feel the twinges of excitement start to peek around the shield to my heart.

Now, if you're not a military wife, let me explain. One of the basic core rules of Military Wife Life 101 is: "Never, ever, ever believe something until you see it in writing. And even then, it can change." (And all the military wives nod their heads.)

Surely the Lord knew how much I needed my husband home, right?

In other words, be on your guard. Don't get your hopes up—not until he's standing right in front of you, in your arms.

But I broke my rule. The higher-ups in Cliff's unit assured him the majority of the battalion was going home, and he was on that list. Cliff assured me he was on that list. For six weeks, we believed he was on the list. We were excited as we planned a possible surprise homecoming, since our son didn't know, and we thought about all the things Cliff was going to be around for, like Valentine's Day and birthdays.

Leading up to the day the list was announced, I'd prayed hard because I knew something could always change. Surely the Lord knew how much I needed my husband home, right? How much Caleb really needed his dad? Surely we'd spent enough time apart with these deployments? Hadn't we done enough time?

Cliff sent me a quick text the morning the list came out. I was getting ready for bed, ten hours behind him.

"Face time?" was all it said.

My heart started beating that nervous, not-sure-what-might-be-happening tap. *Maybe he just wants to see my face when he tells me the good news,* I thought. But as we both came online and I saw his face, I knew something was wrong.

"The list came out," he said. I could tell he was choosing his words carefully. "The majority of the ones here are going home. But another list came out too. And I'm on that list. I'm leaving Afghanistan, but I'm not coming home."

He was headed to another country, a friendlier one in terms of level of physical danger, but still in the Middle East and nowhere near the USA.

I wish I could tell you I took the news like a strong military wife would, with a smile and a quick, "Well, we just push our plans back three months. What's your new address going to be?" But that's not what happened. Instead, all I could do was sob into my hands, my body shaking but no sound escaping. Minutes passed. How desperately I needed his hug at that moment. But all he could do was look helplessly from the other side of the screen, the other side of the world.

"I'm sorry," he said quietly, the pain I was feeling evident on his face too. "They had this new project come up and there are new requirements and not everybody fits the requirements and has the qualifications and I do, and so they need me to go."

I looked at him, my video reflection in the corner of the screen, and I tried to ignore the blotchy redness around my eyes.

"I took off my flak jacket," I said, trying to put it into terms he might understand. "You told me it was OK to take off my flak jacket. You told me it was OK to let my guard down, that this was almost over, and now what you're saying is I have to put it back on for three more months. And I don't want to. I was ready for you to come home and for us to be together again and do normal things, like watch television and get annoyed with the dogs and argue over whose turn it is to do the dishes. I broke the rule. I broke the rule every military wife knows not to break, and now I have to put my flak jacket back on."

> "You told me it was OK to take off my flak jacket. You told me it was OK to let my guard down."

I knew he was just as disappointed as I was. I knew he was ready to come home. It hurt to know there were guys in his battalion who wanted to stay but couldn't because they didn't have the right credentials, but my husband, who was ready to come home, had to stay. I didn't understand. Well, I did in my head. In my heart, all I wanted to do was cry.

> In my heart, all I wanted to do was cry.

For about a week, that's what I did. I'd tear up at just the thought we'd been so close to an early homecoming. They say military wives hold down the fort; that's not exactly what happens. I think a better description is that you hold everything up. Whether you try to or not, you carry everything on your shoulders—the house, the kids, the responsibilities, the communications with your husband, the support and prayers you pass on for him, and you don't even realize the weight you carry until he comes home and you feel it slide off your shoulders.

At least that's what I've experienced. Your heart feels lighter the moment he calls and tells you he's officially back on US soil, the moment he steps off a plane and stands right in front of you. Even the moment a few days later when he's standing in your kitchen helping make dinner and joking around with your son. And you can run off that feeling for months.

I was ready for that relief. I was more than ready for that homecoming. So there were quite a few heated conversations with God during that week following my husband's news. I think that week is probably the most frustrated I've ever felt with God. Was he teaching me a lesson, giving me back the words I'd said just a few weeks before, that I needed my husband home? Was he trying to remind me that he was all I really needed? Isn't that what I've written in Bible studies and what I've shared with other military wives?

> Why couldn't God give me just this one little answer, the way I needed him to answer?

I understood the logic behind that statement that he is all I need, but my feelings were having trouble catching on. I missed my husband. I was tired of missing my husband. Why couldn't God give me just this one little answer, the way I needed him to answer?

Have you been there? Have you lived with or faced great disappointment, maybe even major heartache, and you've known the frustration of calling out to God but unsure if he's actually listening? I would guess, over a lifetime, many of us have and will experience this. There will always be things that happen we can't explain, things we don't like, situations we really wish and pray wouldn't occur. Circumstances and moments we can't blame anyone else for but God because he's the only one who might possibly intervene and make our stress or our heartache go away.

Being angry with God doesn't help heal our hearts, though. Instead, it's a lot like the time I had to go in for a hearing test, and the woman put me in a special booth with a chair and headphones. When she closed the door, there was this absolute stillness of silence.

The only way I could hear her voice was by wearing the headphones. As I closed my eyes, listening for the beeps I knew were coming, I noticed the silence. Sometimes I could hear the sounds come through, but there were also prolonged moments when I couldn't hear anything. There was no sound. No squeak. No beep. Just silence. Uncomfortable, difficult silence. I knew there was something I needed to hear, but as hard as I strained to listen, I couldn't hear anything at all.

> When we get mad at God, we put ourselves in isolation.

When we get mad at God, we put ourselves in isolation. We put ourselves in time-out. Our feelings close us up, preventing us from hearing anything he has to say. Sometimes other emotions have the same effect. We can get angry, but we can also feel fear. Adam and Eve experienced that. Think about it—they had never known what sin was, but as soon as they acted on it, as soon as they'd behaved in a way that disobeyed God, they ran.

> Then the man and his wife heard the sound of the LORD God walking in the garden at the time of the evening breeze, and they hid themselves from the LORD God among the trees of the garden (Genesis 3:8).

They were afraid, afraid of the consequences of their sin.

When we separate ourselves from God, we prolong our problem and we delay the restoration that comes with forgiveness—God's forgiveness of us. We keep our relationships with our heavenly Father at arm's length, and we miss out on his wisdom. We miss out on his grace. We cannot hear his voice.

The mistake in getting angry with God is that only he is our true source for help and for peace and for receiving what we need. When we cut him off, we put ourselves in a difficult position. We tell ourselves he is worse for us than better, and we believe he does more damage in our lives than good.

But this is just wrong. Our anger is wrong.

I don't believe it's wrong to ask questions of God, though some in certain Christian circles do. While others view questions as signs of weak faith or shaky trust, I think God *wants* us to ask our *why* and our *what* and to look for and expect and wonder, because it draws us closer to him.

Recently, I had lunch with some friends after church, and the gal who was hosting us, a fairly new Christian, asked if we might agree that God didn't give us in the Bible all the answers to our questions so we would have a reason to search those answers out and to search him out. So we would have a reason to pursue him. So we wouldn't run or avoid him as he pursues us.

Proverbs 29:11 says that a "fool gives full vent to his anger, but a wise man holds it in check." Another verse in Proverbs says that a "man who does not control his temper is like a city whose wall is broken down" (25:28). A city missing its protective perimeter is a city whose enemies run amok within, and that isn't what we want when we're struggling with anger at God.

Why I Can't Be Angry with God

But let's talk for a moment about why it's a bad idea to be angry with God in the first place.

When we allow ourselves to get angry with God, or to blame God for something that's happened, we ignore the truth we find in Scripture that God desires our best, that he wants us not just to be happy but to be holy. When we become angry with God because of bad or disappointing moments in our lives, we deny that God can work through the bad and we proclaim, mistakenly, that he's around only in the good. Ecclesiastes 7:14 says, "In the day of prosperity be joyful, but in the day of adversity, consider: God has made the one as well as the other."

Even in the hardest, most disappointing moments of our lives, if we believe God loved us enough to send his Son to die on a cross for us, shouldn't we also believe he loves us enough that he doesn't allow unsatisfying or upsetting moments to occur by chance or a plan of his choosing simply because he's out to get us?

That's what other people do. That's not what God does. God is holy and good, and he doesn't play games. He doesn't hold crooked agendas; he doesn't manipulate. He just *is*. He's God, he's Creator, and he's our Lord.

> God is holy and good, and he doesn't play games. He doesn't hold crooked agendas; he doesn't manipulate.

I went through a season of my life where I thought the word *Lord* might be old-fashioned, one of those church words I wasn't sure I should keep using. How silly and utterly wrong I was. When you commit your life to Christ, you commit your life to the Lord.

This word is used throughout God's Word in a couple of different ways. *Lord* is the English translation of the Hebrew word *Adonai*, which means God is our ruler and master. We are dependent on him. He calls the shots; we follow. While we need to have great sensitivity and awareness of the human slavery problem in our world today, we should not be sensitive in our willingness to see ourselves as slaves of Christ.

LORD (in upper and lowercase capital letters in most English Bibles) is also used to translate God's personal name, rendered in Hebrew as *Yahweh* and shared first with Moses. It describes God's role as Father and Redeemer of his children and how unique and endless is his love and his care for us. He is always present with his people. He is faithful and he loves us.

> How I yearn to come to a point in my life where I have completely stripped myself of any interest in what I want.

How I yearn to come to a point in my life where I have completely stripped myself of any interest in what I want, and I am wholly and fully absorbed in living for him in my words, my actions, my thoughts. I'm not sure if this will ever happen in my lifetime, but I know if I want to come close, I must recognize Christ not just as my Savior—who saved me from hell, who prepared a place for me with him in heaven—but also as my Lord, my first thought when I wake up and my last word before I go to sleep.

Jesus.

Lord of all, and Lord of me.

Lord of you.

I can be confident of God's lordship over my life because I trust and live by his Word. There has to be a standard we follow, and I believe that standard must be and can only be the Bible, which is God's Word and has authority over our lives. This is what the Bible says about God and who he is as Lord:

He is great and mighty, showing no partiality (Deuteronomy 10:17).

He keeps his promises (Daniel 9:4).

He bears our burdens (Psalm 68:19) and serves as our refuge (Psalm 90:1).

He is faithful and gracious (Psalm 145:13).

He never leaves (Isaiah 26:4).

Why Bad Things Happen to Good People

So what does this mean when it comes to being angry with God?

I think it's futile to stay angry with God. Nothing good comes from it. Nothing helpful happens when we cut ourselves off from the only one who can walk with us through storms that life brings up. But I don't think it's unusual to ask the question that always seems to come up when we feel like we've been wronged, when we haven't had a fair shake, when we're scratching our heads, wondering what God was thinking or why he isn't helping us in our times of need.

> If there was ever a moment when you might be mad at God for allowing something bad to happen, this might be it.

"Why do bad things happen to good people?"

I think about the story I heard of a pregnant woman who was run off the road and killed when a firefighter coming off his shift fell asleep at the wheel on his way home. He wasn't drinking, he hadn't thought he was too tired to drive when he got into his car, but he dozed off before he could make it home, and a beautiful wife and unborn son were taken from their family. Her husband was a pastor, and she left behind a precious little girl, just a toddler, who would never know her mama. If there was ever a moment when you might be mad at God for allowing something bad to happen, this might be it.

But I was struck at the husband's response in a video I watched online that was shot a few years after he lost his wife. The main theme behind the video was forgiveness, and the unique thread to the story was that he and the man who had accidentally killed his wife and unborn son were now friends.

"There's a bigger picture going on," the husband said. "We have a tendency to look at our lives as three-by-five snapshots, and we can lose sight of the fact that God is doing bigger things in the world, that his story is bigger than ours.

"This isn't a rainbow and butterfly kind of story. There have certainly been a lot of lonely nights and tremendous pain. Thoughts of uncertainty, frustration. Not a day goes by I don't wish my wife was still here. But through it all God has been with me.

"I never would have wanted to endure what I went through, and I never want to feel that way again, but I am who I am today because of what God has done in me through these circumstances, and for that I'm grateful. God is faithful—when our little bit of faith intersects with his faithfulness, God shows up big and does some amazing things in us and through us."

This man had every reason in the world to be angry, certainly with the man who brought harm to his family and perhaps even with God. As a pastor, hadn't he already given so much of his life to God for ministry? Hadn't he served God in so many ways? Had God really needed to take his wife and unborn child?

I'm so thankful this man had the faith and understanding that our God is bigger than we can explain sometimes, and that it's not so much about our story as it is about God's. We are simply part of his narrative.

God created a world that was very good. Genesis 1:31 tells us it was. God isn't responsible for the evil and suffering we find in our world today, but he does give us a choice, and because we humans often choose to be selfish or unkind or uncaring or just plain hateful—bad things happen to good people. Even natural disasters can be attributed to the sin that entered with Adam and Eve. Romans 8:22 says, "For we know that the whole creation has been groaning together with labor pains until now." All of us wait for God's redemption to happen, because ultimately, we're all sinners in need of a Savior (Romans 3:23).

> So what do we do when bad things happen? Do we get angry with God? Or do we praise him anyway?

So what do we do when bad things happen? Do we get angry with God? Or do we praise him anyway? Can we recognize that our lives are not our own and take the humble position a wife did at the bedside of her husband, who lost his battle with cancer, as she raised her hands in praise to God anyway? I'm sure she didn't feel like it; I'm sure her heart was torn in two. And yet, she came to God in the most violent moment of her storm and recognized he was Lord of her life and Lord of her husband's life. What an incredibly moving image of a soul surrendered.

Come as You Are

One of my favorite songs to sing when I was younger was "Come Just as You Are." It's a sweet, simple song with a very powerful message that God wants you to come to him with whatever you're carrying.

There is such importance in that word *come*. You can't come to him when you're angry with God. You're more likely to run when you're in that state of mind, and that isn't what God desires for you. He loves you so much. He wants to help you with your hurt and restore what's broken inside. But he can't do it when you lock yourself away in the isolation booth, unwilling to come out, or you're refusing to pick up the headphones to hear what he has to say.

Won't you let the anger go? Won't you move on from what's been holding you frozen in place?

Won't you surrender?

Here is what I've learned about what it means to surrender, and it isn't easy. I would say it's a similar experience to what happens when you ask God to teach you patience—suddenly, everything that happens to you requires a whole lot of persistence and endurance and a supernatural ability to overlook the stuff that drives you crazy.

Every year, when January 1 rolls around, many of us enjoy choosing a word for the year, a word hopefully we've prayed about and let God lead us in picking. This year I prayed, fully expecting a word like *focus* or *commitment* or *discipline* (because that was my word a couple of years ago, and I'm pretty sure I didn't learn that one as well as I could have).

But I sensed nothing from God except silence. So I thought maybe it was another word like *ready* or *passion* or *pursue*. I didn't feel a peace about any of those.

So I kept praying, straining, trying to hear or understand just what word God might have for me to apply. Then it came to me: *surrender*. And I wanted to give it back.

Surrender? Who wants to surrender? Why

> Surrender? Who wants to surrender? Why not *run* or *fight* or *press on*?

not *run* or *fight* or *press on*? I could think of lots of great Bible verses that would apply to those words.

But that's not what the Lord wanted for me this year, and he had one specific Scripture passage in mind.

> Humble yourselves, therefore, under the mighty hand of God, so that He may exalt you at the proper time, casting all your care on Him, because He cares about you.
>
> Be serious! Be alert! Your adversary the Devil is prowling around like a roaring lion, looking for anyone he can devour. Resist him and be firm in the faith, knowing that the same sufferings are being experienced by your fellow believers throughout the world.
>
> Now the God of all grace, who called you to His eternal glory in Christ Jesus, will personally restore, establish, strengthen, and support you after you have suffered a little (1 Peter 5:6-10).

Just now, I read over that last verse, and God gave me a little nudge. I think about the weariness I've felt lately and the disappointment with waiting for my husband to come home. I think about the other things that have happened these last ten months that have upset me or hurt me or made me just want to bury my head under the covers and not come out. We do suffer, but we also have a *promise*—that God will restore, establish, strengthen, and support us afterward. We have hope in those words.

I hope reading these words of Peter give both you and me the assurance and encouragement that God doesn't cause our suffering—we have an enemy who does that, and his goal is to separate as many of God's children from him as he can. We can't let him win.

Though it sounds counterintuitive, surrendering our lives to God allows him to step in and give us the strength and the heart and the focus we need to carry out what he asks us to do. But we have to humble ourselves. This life isn't about us—it's about God and what he can do through us and with us to bring glory and credit to his name.

But he doesn't leave us hanging. He lifts us up at the proper time. He brings us nourishment to sustain us and give us energy as he did with Elijah, he offers shade to our foreheads as he did with Jonah, he stays by our sides as he did with Joseph, and he rescues us from death just as he did with Lazarus.

Have you ever tried floating in water? Sometimes the more you try moving your arms and legs to stay on top, the more difficult it is to keep from sinking. But what happens when you lie back, breathe, stretch your arms out, lift your face to the sky, and calmly allow the water to hold you up? You float, and you are now in the beautiful position of surrender.

> God, here is all of me. Here is what I have. Here is what I am.

That's what surrendering to God's plan and his purpose looks like. Stretching out, facing him, and saying, "God, here is all of me. Here is what I have. Here is what I am. I'm coming as I am and asking you to use me."

As scary as it can feel to surrender, to stretch out our arms and feel like we've just put ourselves into the most vulnerable position we can, that's when we're the strongest! I can look back at specific times in my life and see what God did when I let go, what he achieved when I stopped trying so hard, what he accomplished when I no longer tried to take on life by myself.

So yes, we are going to suffer. We are going to see disappointment and feel loss and hurt and yes, sometimes even anger when situations seem unfair and not right. But God does not leave us to suffer by ourselves. He doesn't ignore us or forget about us.

If you feel that way, when those lies press in and attempt to convince you that God doesn't love you, that he wants nothing good for you, hold fast to those words in 1 Peter 5:10. Memorize them and let God's promise be your prayer that you will see him work in your life in the days ahead.

That might sound easier to say than actually do, but take a moment and consider Paul, one of the greatest heroes of the faith. For all of his work, for all of the time he spent preaching the gospel of Christ, sharing with others, encouraging people to follow Jesus— Paul did not have an easy life.

He was jailed multiple times and beaten, he was shipwrecked, and he was stoned. People rejected him and his message about Christ, he experienced homelessness and hunger and thirst, and yet none of that stopped him. None of the pain, the hurt, the discouragement, the disappointment, none of the suffering kept him from saying this: "For our momentary light affliction is producing for us an absolutely incomparable eternal weight of glory. So we do not focus on what is seen, but on what is unseen. For what is seen is temporary, but what is unseen is eternal" (2 Corinthians 4:17-18).

> There is no bargain with God; there's only love, there's only hope, there's only grace.

We get angry with God when we buy into the false premise that God has it out for us, or he isn't fulfilling some kind of bargain we've made with him. But there is no bargain with God; there's only love, there's only hope, there's only grace. And if Paul could see that getting locked up and beaten and rejected were only "light afflictions" because he was headed to a much greater reward, surely we can learn to see our troubles and our struggles in the same way.

Like that humble pastor and husband and father who chose to recognize God's bigger picture even in the immense sorrow of losing his wife and child, we can look for the bigger picture in our own situations, in our troubling circumstances, knowing God is for our good, and he loves us and wants his best for us, which is not always the same as our idea of what's best for us.

As you are reading, I hope you're thinking about your relationship with God, and if there is anything you've clung to—if there is any anger or hurt that you're allowing to keep you isolated from him—I hope that you are realizing you don't need to hold on to those things anymore.

I encourage you to read Psalm 103 as we close this chapter. This is one of my favorite psalms in the Bible because it is such a beautiful description and reminder of the grace God pours out onto us every day. Please don't skim through these words, but read them prayerfully, asking God to help you see his reflection and his truth. He is a forgiving God. Will you listen?

Psalm 103

My soul, praise Yahweh,
and all that is within me, praise His holy name.
My soul, praise the LORD,
and do not forget all His benefits.

He forgives all your sin;
He heals all your diseases.
He redeems your life from the Pit;
He crowns you with faithful love and compassion.
He satisfies you with goodness;
your youth is renewed like the eagle.

The LORD executes acts of righteousness
and justice for all the oppressed.
He revealed His ways to Moses,
His deeds to the people of Israel.
The LORD is compassionate and gracious,
slow to anger and rich in faithful love.
He will not always accuse us
or be angry forever.
He has not dealt with us as our sins deserve
or repaid us according to our offenses.

For as high as the heavens are above the earth,
so great is His faithful love
toward those who fear Him.
As far as the east is from the west,
so far has He removed
our transgressions from us.
As a father has compassion on his children,
so the LORD has compassion on those who fear Him.
For He knows what we are made of,
remembering that we are dust.

As for man, his days are like grass—
he blooms like a flower of the field;
when the wind passes over it, it vanishes,
and its place is no longer known.
But from eternity to eternity
the LORD's faithful love is toward those who fear Him,
and His righteousness toward the grandchildren
of those who keep His covenant,
who remember to observe His precepts.
The LORD has established His throne in heaven,
and His kingdom rules over all.

Praise the LORD,
all His angels of great strength,
who do His word,
obedient to His command.
Praise the LORD, all His armies,
His servants who do His will.
Praise the LORD, all His works
in all the places where He rules.
My soul, praise Yahweh!

Five Ways to Let Go of Your Anger
Toward God Right Now

1. **Realize you have a choice.** No one makes you angry with God. You choose that feeling, and when you allow resentment to separate you from God, to build up a wall of your own making, you choose a form of bitterness over his love. Don't be bitter. Don't throw away the goodness of God in your life. Sometimes when we say we're angry with God, we're really just afraid he can't do anything about our hurts. Choose to give your pain to God.

> He will wipe away every tear from their eyes.
> Death will no longer exist;
> grief, crying, and pain will exist no longer,
> because the previous things have passed away.
> (Revelation 21:4)

2. **Look for truth in the situation.** When we're angry or upset with someone else, there's often some truth to why we're upset. But when we're angry with God, it's usually because of a lie we're accepting as truth. Maybe we think if God loved us enough, bad things wouldn't happen, or if God were really as all-powerful as his Word says, a close family member wouldn't be so sick or a friend wouldn't have died. But we can't hold these kinds of statements up to the Bible, our standard, and see them as accurate.

   God doesn't make mistakes. He doesn't hold grudges. What he does is right and good. Our incomplete comprehension of who God is sometimes makes it harder for us to understand what he does and why he does it. When you find yourself getting frustrated with God's action or lack of action, as interpreted by your own observations, pull out Scripture that reminds you of who God truly is. Here are some verses to get you started:

Jeremiah 10:10—He's the true God, the living God, and the "eternal King."

Isaiah 45:18—He alone is God, and there is no other.

Hebrews 4:16—We can come to God with confidence and find mercy and grace in him alone.

Isaiah 26:4—We can trust in God forever because he is everlasting.

Jeremiah 23:24—We cannot hide from God.

3. **Ask questions.** You may have grown up in a family or a church where your faith or even your very salvation was suspect if you ever questioned God. But Job was a man who by God's own admission had done nothing wrong, and he still experienced great personal problems and questioned God about them. So go ahead—ask the hard questions. Write those questions out in a journal, if it helps. Write out your thoughts to God while you're there. Let your questions form into prayers, and understand God wants to listen to it all because he shows his love and his grace to his children. Ask him for deeper understanding as well.

4. **Reinforce your trust.** At some point, through some circumstance or situation in your life, God showed you he is trustworthy. Think of those times when you trusted him with everything, and he provided what you needed. God doesn't change. He is the same God who provided for you then, and he will still provide for you now. Psalm 118:8 says, "It is better to take refuge in the LORD than to trust in man." That means it's better to trust in God than in ourselves too.

5. **Pray.** Just as it's hard to stay mad at someone you keep praying for, it's hard to stay mad at God when you hold that line of communication open through prayer. Prayer builds our faith,

it builds our trust, and it helps keep our perspective where it needs to be.

God is God. He is sovereign and he is in control. We are not. So when we allow ourselves to get mad at God, we're saying we don't trust God enough to lead us, to provide for us, to understand our needs. But we know from his Word that he does, and we must take that to heart. We must believe.

10

Where Love Finds You

When I was a kid, there was a moment where you could almost always find me, if you were looking, scrunched down on the floor behind one of our dining room chairs, my back pressed against the wall, my knees pulled up into my chest, my head tilted toward our kitchen, which was directly on the other side.

This was before the days of cell phones and wireless phones, and in our house, we had the kitchen phone and a phone upstairs in my parents' bedroom. By the time I was ten, we had moved a couple of times (of what would become several moves) for my dad's job, and every week, usually on Sunday afternoons, my mom would call her friends from places where we'd lived to catch up and reconnect.

That's where I would be, hiding around the corner, listening for the words. The words that told me my mother loved me.

My mom often said she loved us, but she was raising three kids in a marriage that wasn't ideal, and so there were times in my childhood I didn't always feel those words. Head and heart can sometimes have trouble interpreting the same information, and like a lot of households, there were some hard moments in our house growing up.

When I think about my mom and how she raised us, there is no doubt in my mind she loved us, and she did the absolute best she could with what she had to give. My mom was a woman who fought for her kids—and still fights for us today as adults, more by prayer than when we were younger since she can't send her infamous letters to our teachers like she once did. She fought for us, but she also fought with us sometimes, and so in my memories there's a cloudy mix of love shaken with some anger and stirred by harsh words.

But when my mom got on the phone with her friends, almost always I could depend on her to tell great stories about her kids—funny stories, impressive stories—and since I was the oldest, those stories were often about me.

She'd talk about all the things I was doing in school, my latest accomplishments, whether it was making the honor roll or starting a club, what I was working on with my music because I was always taking piano lessons or voice lessons or trying out for a part in choir. I remember feeling so much love in those moments, knowing she was so proud of me, and I would look hard for other things I could do. I would work even harder to excel, to accomplish, because I wanted to hear her praise.

I wanted to feel her love.

> The bitterness and the resentment and the negative feelings so many of us struggle with day-to-day can be broken down to the bare necessity of love. Everyone needs love.

I think the bitterness and the resentment and the negative feelings so many of us struggle with day-to-day can be broken down to the bare necessity of love. Everyone needs love. Studies show babies don't thrive if they're not loved when they're very little. When we get hurt, or when we're disappointed or let down, it's tempting to wonder if the people we love the most actually love us back. I think Satan uses these feelings to punch holes into our relationships as well as our hearts, convincing us that people don't really care, that friends and family don't notice, don't listen, and they won't be there for us when we need them to be. The lack of love we perceive is often what increases our lack of trust and our lack of willingness to open up, to connect, and to love back. I think for those reasons, it's hard to forgive when someone hurts us or lets us down.

Don't you wish it were easy to love everyone and everything? Don't you wish it were easy for everyone to love you? There would be no bullies during your elementary years, no cliques in high school to try to fit in or compete with, no slights or snippiness from other adults at your job or at the grocery store or even at church.

We'd all just get along.

But you already know it's not that way, and for all the love we find in the world, there's a whole lot of pain too. Orphans in third-world countries. Famines and wars and political and governmental unrest. Crime. People cheating other people. People hurting other people. Closer to home, the relationships you struggle with and wish could be better. All the expectations we put on others and how often those go unmet. The disappointments, the heartaches, the struggles, the hurt.

I hope you're realizing as you've read that forgiveness is not really about other people. Sure, we want to make it about them—because of what they did or didn't do. But we can't control other people. We can't make them do or say or behave the way we want them to. We *can* make the right choices in our own lives. We don't have to hold on to the pain or the hurt, and we don't have to allow those things to drive wedges into our relationships.

> Full, complete love can really come from only one source. And his name is Jesus.

I think we struggle the most with hurt when we look to everyone and everything else for our love, for our peace, and for our contentment. But full, complete love can really come from only one source. And his name is Jesus.

You might be thinking that's easy to say but a whole lot harder to do. And I agree. But let's look at the love God showed for us through his Son. Let's look at the description the prophet Isaiah gives us of what Jesus went through for us.

> But He was pierced because of our transgressions,
> crushed because of our iniquities;
> punishment for our peace was on Him,
> and we are healed by His wounds.
>
> (Isaiah 53:5)

Paul talks in Ephesians about the incredible quality of Christ's love for us and stresses the importance of knowing "the Messiah's love that surpasses knowledge, so [we] may be filled with all the fullness of God" (Ephesians 3:19).

When we feel filled up to the brim with God's love, grace, and mercy, we can let go of the junk because there's no room for it anyway—we're already full of his love.

This is the secret to forgiveness. When we feel filled up to the brim with God's love, grace, and mercy, those things also pour out of us, and we can let go of the junk because there's no room for it anyway—we're already full of his love.

Jesus talks about this in Matthew 22, quoting Moses who shared this truth with the Israelites as God shared it with him. Jesus says, "Love the Lord your God with all your heart, with all your soul, and with all your mind. This is the greatest and most important command. The second is like it: Love your neighbor as yourself" (22:37-39).

What would it look like if you applied these two verses every single day? What if from the moment you woke up to the minute you lay down, your goal was to carry out these two instructions? Would it change your attitude? Would it change your actions? Would it change your responses to people and circumstances?

Knowing that Jesus was talking to a Pharisee when he shared this absolute truth should also tell us something. Pharisees were notorious for living by the letter of the law, but overlooking God's love, which was at the heart of the law. They were the sheriffs, if you will, for carrying out the traditional forms of the law that had been passed down for generations. They were the ones who started every argument with "We've always done it this way…"

You may know some people like that, people who are great at pointing out everyone's flaws except their own, who are highly offended when something isn't done according to the way it's always been done. Maybe you even fit into this category sometimes.

We may not think of ourselves as rule followers, but I think we can become that way, especially when someone does something we don't like. All of a sudden, we're pointing to our version of life's rule book, insulted and offended that someone crossed the line and hasn't listened, hasn't followed what they're supposed to do.

Why would it be so important to the Lord for us to love our neighbors the way we love ourselves, or the way we want other people to love us? Do you think forgiveness has anything to do with this command?

Sure it does. When we love God with everything we have, and we love other people as we love ourselves, forgiveness becomes natural. When we love God and remember his love for us, we become so wrapped up in his love that forgiving someone else isn't a struggle; it's a joy. When we know our reward and our self-worth are found in Christ, we can overlook the insults or the hurts we experience, because the love of Christ is bigger.

> You reflect to others what your relationship to Christ looks like.

You reflect to others what your relationship to Christ looks like. You reflect to others what God's love looks like to you. And let's go just a bit farther: you reflect to others what God's love looks like *in* you.

This is incredibly convicting to me because when I walk around nursing grudges or bitterness, what do people see of Jesus? When they know I go to church, and I say I love God, and yet they see a frown on my face or they hear me complain and argue and talk negatively about other people—what do they see of God? Yes, you can argue that we're just human and we make mistakes. You're right. But we're also God's children, and we were created in his image. We are reflections of him.

So what are we reflecting?

I think about the times I let my son go places with other people—maybe with other family members like his uncle or his nana or his grammy, or now that he's older, off on trips with our church's youth group—and I hold my breath hoping he does what he's supposed to, he lives out what he's been taught, that he isn't rude or doesn't make bad choices or *make his parents look bad.* Oh, how I would be in trouble if God applied those same thoughts toward me.

John writes in his first epistle that we can be sure we know Christ when we keep his commands, and he's pretty clear on what it means if we don't: "The one who says, 'I have come to know Him,' yet doesn't keep His commands, is a *liar,* and the truth is not in him. But whoever keeps His word, truly in him the love of God is perfected. This is how we know we are in Him: The one who says he remains in Him *should walk just as He walked*" (1 John 2:4-6, emphasis mine).

So this is our challenge. After everything we've discussed in these chapters about letting go, about overcoming hurt, releasing pain, letting scars heal, maybe now it's time to focus less on the reflection and more on the source of our hope, the source of our life, the source of our love. Let's leave the white noise behind and start listening for his voice, his hope, his truth.

Let's move past the question, *What about me?* and instead apply the question, *What about him?*

Let's worry less about our rights and worry more about sharing his good.

Let's stop holding grudges against the things that go wrong in our lives, or the people who disappoint us, and instead, let's focus on his grace.

Let's give others extra chances because we recognize the extra chances God gives us.

Let's be intentional in showing love to other people, knowing God shows his love to us each and every day.

Intensional Love

So let me go back to the question I asked earlier: What would it look like to love God with everything you have? How do you show love to your neighbor, the person who annoys you, or the person who hurt you?

> What would it look like to love God with everything you have?

I think we do it with *intensional* love—love with intensity. Here's what I mean by that. If you look at 1 Peter 4, he spends a great deal of time in that chapter talking to the early church on how to reflect more of Jesus in their lives and with each other.

Start with Prayer

The first thing he says is that we need to be "serious and disciplined for prayer" (1 Peter 4:7). Intensional love must start with prayer. I've mentioned this previously in the context of forgiveness, but it certainly applies when we're discussing love. Let's face it—most people will have unlovable moments, especially the individuals we struggle to forgive. So we have to start with prayer.

I know this is difficult for a lot of people. I once asked a group of military wives to join me at our usual meeting time, but instead of Bible study, we would spend some time praying for each other and for our families. I had one person come, and she admitted right away how nervous she was to pray because she never knew what to say. Even praying by herself, just her and God, made her uncomfortable.

But prayer isn't meant to intimidate; it's intended to be a means of communication and communion between us and God. This is one of the most beautiful ways we can spend time in worship as well as an opportunity to

> Praying is simply talking with God as you recognize his authority over your life.

talk to our Creator, and it's so important to actively pray if we want to be able to walk in forgiveness and to live with a mind and heart set on reflecting God's love.

Praying is simply talking with God as you recognize his authority over your life. While I am not a fan of formulas or rote prayers, sometimes it does help to have a starting point you can learn from. If you find yourself struggling to know how to pray or you're self-conscious about what to say, I suggest you try the ACTS model: Adoration, Confession, Thanksgiving, and Supplication—all big words for important components of prayer.

Adoration. Open your prayer with praise for God. Tell him how much you love him. Communicate what you've noticed that he's done, whether in the beautiful sunrise you saw as you rocked your baby in the early morning hours, or the encouragement your coworker gave you that you know God was responsible for.

Confession. Confess or acknowledge before the Lord anything that you've done wrong. (He already knows what those things are, so there's no use in denying them.) Don't be general or offer generic statements like "I'm sorry if I've done anything wrong." Be specific and thank him for the forgiveness we have only through Christ.

Thanksgiving. There is so much to thank God for. Thank him for dying on the cross for your sins, thank him for providing for you and your family, thank him for the specific ways you've seen him work in your life.

> But God wants us to ask for what we and others we are praying for need. Nothing is insignificant to him.

Supplication. This is a fancy word that means to ask or beg in earnest for what you and others need, with humility. I think sometimes we struggle to ask for what we need because we're afraid of the answer (or lack of answer) we might get from God. But God wants us to ask for what we and others we are praying for need. Nothing is insignificant to him. Make your requests known.

Be Intensional in Your Love

"Above all, maintain an intense love for each other, since love covers a multitude of sins" (1 Peter 4:8). We need to be both intentional and intense with showing love to one another. We're talking about being earnest or serious and without ceasing, without stopping. We don't give up. Love doesn't quit. God's love doesn't quit and neither should ours, because love wins over hate. Love wins over bitterness. Love wins over whatever offends us.

What happens when you're kind toward someone else? Do you typically feel worse? Or better? If we could apply more intensional love to our situations and circumstances, I think a big portion of the issues that require forgiveness or letting things go would go away.

First John 4:18-19 says, "There is no fear in love; instead, perfect love drives out fear, because fear involves punishment. So the one who fears has not reached perfection in love. We love because He first loved us."

God's love transforms us, and when we trust his love, we can let go of the selfishness and the self-preservation we so often want to keep close by, ready to pull out when life gets too hard or relationships get too messy. Living out his love with intension, though, means getting messy and taking risks of getting hurt. But we can do it because he was willing to get messy first.

> If we can't love the people we see in the flesh, then we can't love God, who we can't see at all.

Be Hospitable

In 1 Peter 4:9, the Greek word for "hospitable" (*philoxenia*) means "love of strangers," and makes me immediately think of 1 John 4:20-21 which says (I'm paraphrasing) that if we can't love the people we see in the flesh, then we can't love God, who we can't see at all.

I think the importance of hospitality is overlooked in some churches today, and I wonder if it's because many of us are so much busier than we used to be, or at least we perceive that we're busier.

Frankly, it's also that our choices and our priorities have changed. If it's not with our jobs or our spouses' jobs, then it's the activities with our kids. We no longer have any margin or space in our schedules to look out for one another.

Case in point: In recent weeks, as I've been locked away, working hard to finish this book while still juggling responsibilities with my son, my ministry, and just daily life, a sweet friend of mine had her baby, and I found out a week after the fact that she'd experienced complications after the birth. During the same time frame, another friend was dealing with going back to a new job after giving birth to her second child, and still another friend had a child who was very sick and her own health wasn't in the best shape. But because I was so busy—I had no time to help or be the hands and feet of Jesus to any of them.

We're called to serve others, and when we make the choice to focus less on our wants or needs, those moments of service allow us to be more present and more aware of what God wants us to do to make his name known. To do that, though, we have to be intentional, and we have to have time to look for those opportunities to serve. Saying we wish we could have helped isn't the same as actually helping.

> If you know Christ, you're called to serve and minister to the people around you.

Use Your Spiritual Gifts

When we ask God for our next assignment, we will be less sensitive to what others are or aren't doing for us and more sensitive to what the Holy Spirit is leading us to do. "Based on the gift each one has received, use it to serve others, as good managers of the varied grace of God" (1 Peter 4:10). Pastors and missionaries aren't the only ones called to ministry. If you know Christ, you're called to serve and minister to the people around you, and you can start by making use of the gifts God's given you. Spiritual gifts are supernatural—they are abilities we can't learn on our own, or from school, but instead, are given by God not for our benefit but for the benefit of all believers.

We find roughly sixteen different spiritual gifts listed in the following Bible passages: Romans 12:6-8; 1 Corinthians 12:8-19,28-30; Ephesians 4:11-13; 1 Peter 4:9-11. If you're not sure what your spiritual gifts are, visit my website to download a free copy of a *Spiritual Gifts Survey* by Gene Wilke and published by LifeWay Christian Resources (sarahorn.com/spiritualgifts).

Speak God's Words, Serve in God's Strength

Wow, if we thought about what God wanted us to say, before we spoke, how would *that* change our outlook? "If anyone speaks, it should be as one who speaks God's words; if anyone serves, it should be from the strength God provides, so that God may be glorified through Jesus Christ in everything" (1 Peter 4:11). When we are fully settled in God's love, seeking out ways to serve him and to minister to others, he works in our own lives as well, growing us and shaping us into the women he's called us to be.

> If they don't hear about him from you, how will they hear about him?

We live in such a skeptical, guarded world today. So much of what we see we don't like, and I think there's a growing fear and pressure among Christians not to reach out and not to speak, not to share what God's doing in our lives. But people need him now more than ever, and if they don't hear about him from you, how will they hear about him? When we can walk through the challenges of forgiveness, demonstrating God's grace as we pass it on to others, we open doors for opportunities to talk about why we can forgive and why it's not through our own power we can do so.

Free at Last

God's love doesn't fail us. He doesn't forget us, and he never laughs at our expense. But he does desire that we choose him, that we stop being so stubborn and strong-willed and unwilling to accept his grace and in turn, deny that grace to others.

I've learned a lot about letting go of hurts and resentment the last few years, and perhaps the biggest lesson I've learned is that when you let go, you make room for more of God in your life, and little by little he fills you up. Forgiving others and moving on from those difficult situations instead of dwelling on them is a choice. When we choose forgiveness over holding a grudge, we make the better choice.

Poor Martha, the sister in Luke 10 who just wanted to get a good meal on the table for Jesus and could have used a little help, has been vilified for centuries as the one who made the wrong choice. But if we're honest, most of us would be Martha. And not just in the kitchen. I think many of us find it difficult to choose what's not right in front of us. Put another way, it's easier to get caught up in today than remember and focus on tomorrow—and as a follower of Christ, we have tomorrow!

When we choose forgiveness, we choose tomorrow because we recognize that grace gives second chances (and thirds and fourths) for other people as well as for ourselves. Forgiveness heals and restores and overlooks and offers freedom from sin and honest mistakes.

Forgiving other people isn't easy. Letting go of hurt or disappointment isn't like letting go of an old jacket or dress we no longer want, but we still need to get rid of them for similar reasons—we can't afford the space we give up when we hold on to those things.

When we choose forgiveness, we choose life. We choose love, and we choose God's way over our own.

Toward the end of the book of Deuteronomy, we find the Israelites at a certain crossroad in their journey. They've struggled to stay faithful to the Lord in their travels, and they've gone through a lot—escaping Egypt, wandering through the wilderness, and finally making their way back to Canaan, the land

God promised them. As they prepare to enter the territory they've waited for decades to enter, Moses, their leader and their spiritual father, talks to them about where they've been, where they're about to go, and the very important choice they have. He challenges them but he also encourages them, and he stresses that it's not a difficult choice to make.

> See, today I have set before you life and prosperity, death and adversity. For I am commanding you today to love the LORD your God, to walk in His ways, and to keep His commands, statutes, and ordinances, so that you may live and multiply, and the LORD your God may bless you in the land you are entering to possess. But if your heart turns away and you do not listen and you are led astray to bow down to other gods and worship them, I tell you today that you will certainly perish and will not live long in the land you are entering to possess across the Jordan. I call heaven and earth as witnesses against you today that I have set before you life and death, blessing and curse. Choose life so that you and your descendants may live, love the LORD your God, obey Him, and remain faithful to Him (Deuteronomy 30:15-20).

When we choose forgiveness, we choose life. We choose love, and we choose God's way over our own.

When we choose to forgive instead of holding it all in, we willingly let go of all that white noise that might distract. Instead, we choose to listen to the quiet whispers of our heavenly Father speaking into our hearts and lives, reminding us that his grace is sufficient for us. His power and his strength are even stronger in our weaknesses.

Only when we are weak, then are we strong, because we experience and know grace firsthand, and we can pass that grace on to others.

Choose life, my friend. Choose the beauty God offers you today. Choose to live out love in his way, and not yours or anyone else's.

Choose "I forgive you." Choose "I'm sorry." Choose "I'm letting it go."

There is no sweeter sound than the exhale of release. Forgiveness is possible when we give all of it to God.

Five Ways to Live Out Love Right Now

1. **Start each morning in prayer.** Ask God to give you the day he wants you to have, and ask him to help you see the opportunities he puts in your path to show love to others.

2. **Look for one opportunity a day to minister to someone (or make someone's day better).** Whether it's a random act of kindness for a total stranger or encouragement for a friend, find a way to pass God's love on to someone.

3. **Look for the positive.** Too often, it's easy to find the negative, whether in your office, your women's Bible study, or around the other moms at your child's school or homeschool cohort. Commit to speak in love, finding ways to set a new trend of positive, God-honoring conversation.

4. **Show kindness.** Sometimes we are the least kind to the people we live with and love the most. Be proactive in giving compliments or helpful gestures to your immediate family and yes, even to those in your extended family. And if your kindness isn't returned or is simply overlooked? Do it anyway. You're not doing it just for them.

5. **Be ready to show love to others.** Prepare some practical ways of showing love ahead of time, so you're never caught off guard: have a casserole in the freezer ready to be dropped off when someone needs a meal; keep in your wallet a stash of five-dollar gift cards to your favorite fast-food restaurant that you can hand to someone who might be hungry; designate one night a week that anyone in the family can invite guests over for dinner.

Discussion Questions for Journaling or Small Groups

1. If you had to name a specific sound, what would you say forgiveness sounds like to you?

2. Have you ever struggled to forgive someone? How did that struggle affect your life? Or did it?

3. Look in chapter 2 at the list of Seven Habits of Highly Resentful People and Seven Habits of Highly Forgiving People. Which list could you relate to the most? Are there changes you need to make in your life to be more forgiving? If so, what would you say they were?

4. Have you ever been in the wrong and knew it? Was the conflict resolved the way you wanted it to be? Why or why not?

5. Is it hard to forgive when someone says something hurtful or overlooks you? How can you handle this better the next time it happens?

6. Have you ever had a situation where an apology or an act of forgiveness ended in a restored relationship? How did it come about, and what might have happened if forgiveness hadn't occurred?

7. Have you ever been mad at God? How did you get past the anger or frustration?

8. Have you ever held a grudge? What did it do to you, and how were you able to overcome it?

9. After reading this book, is there a situation that God has brought to your mind that you need to let go? How are you going to move on from it?

10. Why is forgiveness so important to us as believers?

Notes

1. Caleb K. Bell, "Poll: Americans Love the Bible But Don't Read It Much," *Religion News Service*, www.religionnews.com/2013/04/04/poll-americans-love-the-bible-but-dont-read-it-much/.

2. Ed Stetzer, "New Research: Less Than 20% of Churchgoers Read the Bible Daily, *Christianity Today*, www.christianitytoday.com/edstetzer/2012/september/new-research-less-than-20-of-churchgoers-read-bible-daily.html.

3. Oswald Chambers, *My Utmost for His Highest*, February 6.

4. Boz Tchividjian, "Startling Statistics: Child Sexual Abuse and What the Church Can Begin Doing About It," *Rhymes with Religion* (blog), http://boz.religionnews.com/2014/01/09/startling-statistics/.

About the Author

Sara Horn is a wife, mom, author, speaker, and founder of Wives of Faith, a ministry to military wives (www.wivesoffaith.org). Since 2006, Sara has encouraged and inspired military wives of all branches of service to seek God's strength over their own. As God has expanded her ministry, her desire is to help women everywhere see their incredible value through God's eyes, know their distinct calling, fulfill their important roles in their families, and develop strong relationships with God.

Sara has written professionally for more than ten years. As the wife of a Navy reservist, she had the rare privilege of traveling to Iraq twice in 2003 to report and write stories of Christians in the military. Her first book, *A Greater Freedom: Stories of Faith from Operation Iraqi Freedom*, recorded those travels and was written with Oliver North, receiving a 2005 Gold Medallion nomination. Her books for the military wife include *GOD Strong* and the Bible study, *Tour of Duty*. Her most recent titles are *My So-Called Life as a Proverbs 31 Wife* and *My So-Called Life as a Submissive Wife*.

Though for many years Sara said she'd never do women's ministry, God had other plans, and he has instilled in her a passion to encourage and speak to the hearts of women, reminding them of the hope and strength we have when we rely on him.

She currently lives in the Baton Rouge, Louisiana, area with her son and her husband, who just recently returned from his third deployment.

To correspond with Sara or to request her to speak at your event, contact her at sara@sarahorn.com or visit her website at sarahorn.com. You may also connect with her on Facebook at facebook.com/sarahornwrites or on Twitter (@sarahorn).

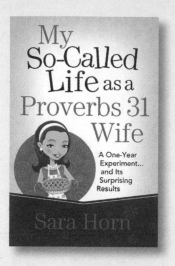

My So-Called Life as a Proverbs 31 Wife
A One-Year Experiment...and Its Surprising Results

Sara Horn always admired the Proverbs 31 wife, but when she became a busy writer and mother, she deemed this model to be dated and impossible. Or is it? Join Sara as she heads into a one-year domestic experiment and offers full access to see if this biblical model can be embraced by a modern woman—even one who can't sew.

With humility and humor, Sara sets out to pursue the Proverbs 31 characteristics through immersing herself in all things domestic. But when her family's situation changes and she must return to a full-time job, she's forced to look at the Proverbs 31 woman with a whole new viewpoint. Through it all, she (and you) will discover:

- what it means to be a godly woman and wife
- how investing in family and faith refines priorities as a spouse and a parent
- how mistakes are opportunities for growth

This thought-provoking, surprising, and entertaining personal account will inspire you to try your own experiments in living out God's purpose for your life.

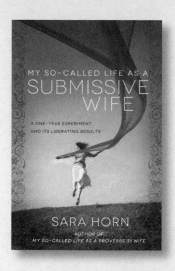

My So-Called Life as a Submissive Wife
A One-Year Experiment...and Its Liberating Results

Can a modern wife be submissive to her husband?

In her highly anticipated sequel to *My So-Called Life as a Proverbs 31 Wife*, Sara Horn takes on one of the most widely debated subjects for a Christian wife—marital submission.

What does biblical submission look like for wives today? And why is *submission* viewed as such a dirty word by so many women and men in our culture, including Christians? Can a happily married couple live out the biblical model of submission and be the better for it?

Horn takes on a one-year experiment to seek answers to these questions and to explore what it means to be submissive as a wife and "helper" to her husband. The answers—and her discoveries—may surprise you.

This unique, entertaining, and thought-provoking personal account will challenge you to throw out your preconceived notions of what a submissive wife looks like and seek fresh leading from God for your life and marriage today.

To learn more about Harvest House books and
to read sample chapters, visit our website:

www.harvesthousepublishers.com

HARVEST HOUSE PUBLISHERS
EUGENE, OREGON